BEST SHORT HIKES

IN WASHINGTON'S

SOUTH CASCADES & OLYMPICS

BEST SHORT HIKES

IN WASHINGTON'S

SOUTH CASCADES & OLYMPICS

E. M. Sterling

Photos by Bob & Ira Spring

THE
MOUNTAINEERS

Founded in 1906, The Mountaineers is a Seattle-based non-profit outdoor activity and conservation club with 15,000 members, whose mission is "to explore, study, preserve, and enjoy the natural beauty of the outdoors . . . ." The club sponsors many classes and year-round outdoor activities in the Pacific Northwest, and supports environmental causes by sponsoring legislation and presenting educational programs. The Mountaineers Books supports the club's mission by publishing travel and natural history guides, instructional texts, and works on conservation and history. For information, call or write The Mountaineers, Club Headquarters, 300 Third Avenue West, Seattle, Washington, 98119; (206) 284-6310.

© 1995 by E. M. Sterling

9 8 7 6 5
5 4 3 2 1

Published by The Mountaineers,
1011 SW Klickitat Way, Seattle, Washington 98134

Published simultaneously in Canada by Douglas & McIntyre, Ltd.,
1615 Venables Street, Vancouver, B.C. V5L 2H1

Published simultaneously in Great Britain by Cordee,
3a DeMontfort Street, Leicester, England, LE1 7HD

Manufactured in the United States of America

Edited by Kris Fulsaas
Maps by Word Graphics
Book typesetting and layout by The Mountaineers Books
All photographs by Bob and Ira Spring except as noted
Cover photograph: Mount Rainier National Park (Hike 41)
Frontispiece: "Hole-in-the-Wall," a natural archway north of Rialto Beach (Hike 21)

Library of Congress Cataloging-in-Publication Data
Sterling, E. M.
Best short hikes in Washington's South Cascades and Olympics / E.M. Sterling ; photos by Bob & Ira Spring.
    p.   cm.
    Includes bibliographical references (p.   ) and index.
    ISBN 0-89886-417-8 (pbk.)
    1. Hiking--Washington (State)--Guidebooks. 2. Hiking--Cascade Range--Guidebooks. 3. Hiking--Washington--Olympic Mountains--Guidebooks. 4. Trails--Washington (State)--Guidebooks. 5. Washington (State)--Guidebooks. 6. Cascade Range--Guidebooks. 7. Olympic Mountains (Wash.)--Guidebooks. I. Title.
GV199.42.W2S745   1994
796.5'1'09797--dc20   94-44879
                                                              CIP

Contents

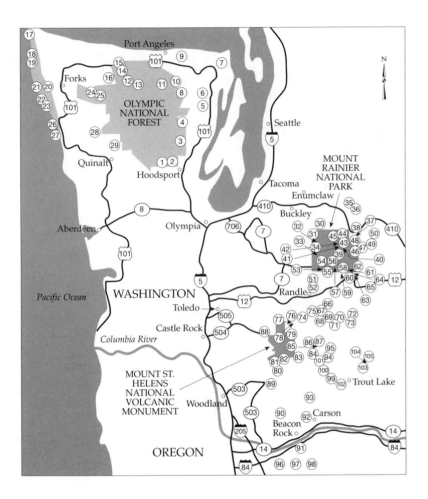

Highway 503 and Road 90
(Woodland to Lewis River Falls)

Spirit Lake Memorial Highway 504
(Interstate 5 to Mount St. Helens)

Highway 503
(Chelatchie to Silver Star Mountain)

Highway 14
(Beacon Rock State Park to Carson)

Oregon Interstate 84
(Columbia Gorge)

Forest Road 88
(Trout Lake)

Forest Roads 23 and 80
(Trout Lake–Yakama Indian Reservation)

MAP LEGEND

————————	Highway, road	\24/	Forest Service road
= = = = = =	Forest Service road	2810	Secondary forest road
- - - - - - - - - -	Trail	⬆	Ranger station, visitor center
—··—··—··—	Boundary	⋀	Campground
～～～	River, creek	▲	Peak, lookout
(90)	Interstate	■	Building
(2)	US highway	][	Bridge
(410)	State highway	)(	Pass

Hall of Mosses in Hoh Rain Forest (Hike 24)

Introduction

If this book of Best Short Hikes has any single purpose it is this: to provide a usable sampler of the best places to hike in the most beautiful forests and parks in the Olympics, around Mount Rainier, in the South Cascades, and in the Columbia River Gorge.

With waterfalls, mountain vistas, wild seashores, high meadows, the splendor of flowers, the exuberance of streams, and even the horrendous powers of a volcano—just to start.

Written for newcomers, most certainly. For people with young families, yes. For hikers with limited stamina and limited time, most certainly. For the many who love the best of nature, of course. And for all and everyone who looks to the Northwest outdoors for moments of re-creation in very busy lives.

With every hike designed to fit within a day as part of a single trip. Stressing, in saying that, that no one-day trip must be limited to a single hike or that a single hike may not be spread over several days. Many of these hikes can be grouped to fit a weekend, a week, and even more.

Campgrounds are listed in the back of the book to help plan any trip of several days.

How to Use This Book

The format here is simple. The hikes are grouped, in order, along highways or major forest roads with a summary of essential information for each hike.

Directions are given to trailheads, and each hike is described, pictured, and mapped (in most instances) on facing pages so that details of each trip can easily be copied and carried. Larger forest, state and national park, Green Trail, Custom Correct, and wilderness maps are identified. Nearby campgrounds are listed in the appendix for groups of hikes in each area.

Maps

Most of the maps suggested here can be purchased at outdoor equipment stores. Maps of national forests (Olympic, Mount Baker–Snoqualmie, Wenatchee, Gifford Pinchot, and Mount Hood) can be obtained at headquarter offices and ranger stations

A helping hand (photo: Kirkendall/Spring)

within each forest for a modest fee. Wilderness maps, likewise, can be purchased at offices in forests in which the wilderness is located. Entrance gates to Olympic and Mount Rainier national parks offer brochures that identify and locate most park trails listed here. U.S. Geological Survey 7.5- and 14-minute maps can also be obtained at map stores.

A note: Some current Green Trail 14-minute maps of areas in the South Cascades may not display up-to-date forest road numbers. Check them against national forest maps.

Trails

Unless otherwise noted, all trails listed are clearly signed and easy to follow. Although an effort has been made to rate the difficulty of each trail, hikers will need to adjust those judgments to fit themselves. (Suffice it to say that eighteen-year-olds and eighty-year-olds have different views of steep.)

Steep or not, many of the trails here may be rough, often muddy and wet, as all mountain trails are wont to be. One-log bridges cross many streams, rock hopping and even wading may sometimes be required. Windfalls and washouts, particularly early in the summer, may make travel difficult or impossible on any trail. If you can, check conditions with rangers before you start.

Roads

Many of the roads listed in this book, particularly in national forests, are gravel roads in various states of repair, disrepair, and non-repair.

At the time this was written, national forests had just begun a program to obliterate roads, generally those no longer used for logging but including many still being used for recreation purposes as access to lakes, flower meadows, vista points, berry fields, other trails, etcetera.

All of the roads were built with public funds and are—or were—therefore public roads. If you find a recreation road that's closed or hear of one that's about to be closed, let forest supervisors know how you feel about that. And why.

Likewise, if you find a recreation road in desperate need of maintenance, speak again. A road fit only for a tractor is not being managed as a "public" road.

And a word about directions: Many of the trails listed here can be reached a number of different ways. Particularly those in the Gifford Pinchot National Forest. If you would like to get from one trail to another without having to return to "go" each time, consult rangers and forest maps to find a better way. Adding another level of adventure to your trip because on forest roads— you can't be sure of anything.

Equipment

Equipment needs for all of these hikes are minimal. Although street shoes will suffice on some of the "easy" trails listed here, hiking shoes are recommended for them all. For all mountain trails can be rough, muddy, and sometimes covered with snow.

Every hiker in the mountains, even on the short hikes listed here, should start every hike prepared, in an emergency, to at least survive the night. Accidents occur in mountains, as in the city, without warning. But in the mountains often no one is nearby to help. There are no 911 telephones waiting in the trees or rocks.

The Mountaineers lists Ten Essentials to be carried on every hiking trip. And we urge them here. These necessities include extra clothing (weather in these mountains can change without notice, even in the summer), extra food, sunglasses, knife, fire-starter, first-aid kit, matches in a waterproof container, flash-light, map, compass.

In a rucksack, certainly.

And yes, take your camera and, if you have them, a flower book, a bird book, and pictures of animal tracks.

Water

Carry water on every hike. Water in none of the streams crossed on these trails, tragically, should nowadays be considered safe to drink unless it has been boiled 5 minutes, filtered, or treated with approved sterilization procedures.

Fires

We discourage the building of campfires on these short hikes. Most of the destinations here where campfires might suggest themselves are already overused and, for firewood, overcut. If you want hot soup or coffee for lunch, carry a small mountain stove that will not only assure your meal but save your destination from further destruction.

Trash and Waste

By all means carry out whatever trash you carry in: paper, bottles, cans. And if you truly want to help, carry out what others may have left.

Use trailside privies when possible. Otherwise, bury your body waste in a shallow hole well away from campsite or trail, and at least 200 feet from streams and other water sources. Burn toilet paper and then cover the waste with soil and leaves.

Dogs

Dogs? Start with no. Pets are barred from trails in national parks. In most other areas they are permitted. But: On trails they frighten wild animals and birds that you or others might see along the trail. And worse, they often frighten hikers too. You may know your dog will not bite, but do I? So make it a rule:

Don't take your dog unless it's necessary. Stressing that the "necessity," in the eyes of others, is yours to defend.

Trailhead Parking

A sad warning about parking at trailheads: Leave nothing of value in your car. Anywhere. Seen or unseen. In the seat or in the trunk. And if you have expensive radio, speaker, or CD gear, don't park at all.

And always look for loiterers when you arrive at a trailhead. Particularly "hikers," or so they may seem, who spend all of their time "getting ready" either to leave or to start a hike. Note a license number if you can, jot down a description of those you see, and, if you return to damage, or find the same "hikers" once again, report it to rangers or law enforcement officers. Sad. How sad.

Campgrounds

Campgrounds in the appendix of this book are listed for groups of trails along main roads. All of the campgrounds listed are operated by local, state, or federal agencies that may charge daily fees for the use of their facilities.

All of the camps include parking and tent areas, picnic tables, and fire pits. All have at least pit toilets. Water is available if indicated.

Space in the campgrounds, however, is not assured. Most of the camps are likely to be filled on weekends and holidays. Best opportunities occur midweek before or after school vacation periods. Reservations may be available for some camps, as noted on current forest maps.

Many non-fee camps do not provide garbage services. In those camps, take yours home. *Please*, take yours home.

And lest we forget: Remember how far sound carries in the woods. Keep your radio turned down and remember that 10:00 P.M. is bedtime in every camp.

So Enjoy—and Learn

And then enjoy? Yes, most certainly. But, more importantly, beyond pleasure, look around you as you hike. See and seek to understand.

While you drive forest roads to trailheads, for example, look closely and with purpose at what you see along the road.

First, in the lower valleys, ask how much of the summer green is brush and alders and how little of it regrowing conifers, of the kind that once grew there. And should—if they'd been re-planted—grow there now.

Later, as your road climbs higher, note the clear-cuts, new and old, and wonder about the impact of what you see. On birds, rodents, deer, or bear. On snowfall runoff in the spring. On the retention of rainfall in the summer. On avalanche control. On the variety of surviving plants. On the health of streams or salmon spawning beds. Even the purity of the air you breathe. Understanding as you make your guess that those who logged those forests took no time to answer any of those questions before doing what you see already done.

And then, while pausing in an ancient forest, ask what trees grow there? What trees don't? What factors—weather, elevation, logging, water—impose the limits you suspect?

Wonder why one forest stands so open and so grand while another is such a tumult of debris. Will some of the big trees you see standing now in open groves have to fall to let still bigger ones claim the forest space? Or will everything collapse at once? And is the snarled forest you see a gain or loss? Is the tumult the result of some disease (most likely not) or of some evolving forest argument over places in the sun in which some win, some lose.

What about the soil on the forest floor? Barren? Rich with duff? Could Indian pipes live without the thick decay from which they rise? Could the monkey flowers beside a stream survive without the water? The trilliums without the shade? The scarlet Gilia without a desert slope?

And the logging sites themselves? Could (should) some of the abandoned debris you see have been utilized? Will those re-planted slopes, stocked as advertised on TV ads with two- or three-foot-high seedlings for every huge old tree cut down, ever—ever—equal the uncut old forests that existed there before? Remembering those you've hiked through from this book.

And what about the gouges etched in a mountainside where felled logs were dragged uphill to trucks? Have they healed? Will they heal? Will the erosion you see there harm salmon spawning grounds on some river far, far below?

Douglas fir at Iron Creek Campground (Hike 74)

And then, would the logged forest you see recover more certainly—and more grandly—if other methods, "practices" of logging, as they say, had been carried out? Like those used in the now recovered selective cuts made early in the century before the chainsaw came. Or like those still so carefully being carried out by every nation in the beautiful forests of alpine Europe.

And what of the roads, now being abandoned, although built

Chanterelle

with tax dollars, because the logging's finished and the forest agency has no money to keep them up? Did you want those roads built with your money for loggers and no one else? Is that what the public expected from promises of multiple use?

In some places where public roads are closed, hikers are being forced (although motorbikers and trailbikers are often not!) to walk longer distances on those barricaded roads to reach the natural forest trails they hiked before. Will the added distance for hikers limit use? By whom? For whom? And if so, why is that?

And from vista points? How many clear-cuts must be ignored to see (enjoy?) the mountain 30 miles away? Is that the best that can be done—should be done—with the forest the public owns?

And the trails? Was this section of trail truly "restored" after the loggers cut all the trees and left? And the ruts you see on steep trails—so narrow and so deep not even elk can walk them anymore—were they created by mountain motorbikes? Permitted on the trail?

And what about those trail machines? If somebody invents and builds some new machine, of any kind, must the public automatically permit its destructive use? On trails? Across virgin meadows? For whatever kicks some buyer wants? What next? Trail bulldozers for the crowd? Toy tanks? Dynamiting kits?

What about the wilderness? Is it possible to maintain a wilderness in a pristine state without totally banning public use? Or should some damage be expected, accepted, and controlled? Privies? Trail signs? Formal camping spots? More off-trail use? Or would more trails, more access points spread out the use?

Or would fewer trails and less access help more? Help whom? Or deny wilderness to how many?

Yes, enjoy what you find here. But, please, accept *responsibility* for everything you see.

For remember: You are the keeper of every forest, private or public, anywhere. You have a personal interest, and a right to have an interest, in every clear-cut, road, unlogged area, replanted site, wilderness, lake, waterfall, and river that you see. Anywhere.

Public forests—and all of them—are yours to manage. For you own them. Every one. It's your money being spent. Your policies being carried out. You deserve credit for what is good, and

Fawn hiding in the Lewis River valley

you also deserve blame for what is bad. For you have received exactly what you asked for. And if you didn't ask? Who else is there to blame?

And on private forests? On those huge ugly logged-off blocks of railroad land? Trees—most of them—cut and shipped to the Orient. You're responsible for those forests too.

Private forests, throughout all of the nations of the western world, including Washington, are forests awarded to private owners to be held and used in trust for you. The public here (in Europe it was once the sovereign king) has, and always has had, the right, the power, the obligation to demand that forests—all forests—be managed in the public (in your, the sovereign's) interest all the time.

And for reasons so ancient and so basic they are sometimes overlooked. Forests are and have been necessary for all people— in the nation, in the world—for housing, recreation, stability of

Thimbleberry

the soil, avalanche control, water retention, weather, even air quality, along with the survival of birds, plants, fish, and animals—just to begin a list.

Therefore, it's in your individual undisputed public interest, as guardian of all forests in a democracy, to impose and enforce all of the necessary practices, controls, and restraints.

For, again, it's your forest—private or public—being saved or wasted. Your rules being enforced or ignored. Your future being thrown away or saved. Yours and yours alone.

So protect your interest. Take part. Insist. Demand.

Join others, yes, who seek the things you seek. Give them your wholehearted support. But also act on your own, speaking for yourself and for your children and grandchildren, born and unborn, directly to those who represent you. And demand, yes, demand, that they respond personally to your requests.

And then? Oh yes. Most certainly. Enjoy!

A Note About Safety

Safety is an important concern in all outdoor activities. No guidebook can alert you to every hazard or anticipate the limitations of every reader. Therefore, the descriptions of roads, trails, routes, and natural features in this book are not representations that a particular place or excursion will be safe for your party. When you follow any of the routes described in this book, you assume responsibility for your own safety. Under normal conditions, such excursions require the usual attention to traffic, road and trail conditions, weather, terrain, the capabilities of your party, and other factors. Keeping informed on current conditions and exercising common sense are the keys to a safe, enjoyable outing.

The Mountaineers

North Fork Skokomish River from Shady Lane trail

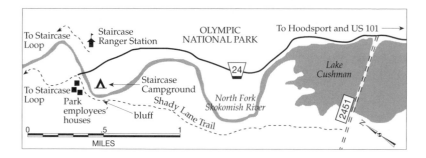

 Shady Lane

Features: forest and cliffs
One way: 1 mile plus
Elevation gain: none
Difficulty: easy
Open: spring to fall
Maps: Green Trails 167; Custom Correct, Skokomish/Cushman

An easy stroll here leads through an old forest and elk range, along the shores of a lake, the bottom of a cliff, and history.

From Hoodsport on US Highway 101, drive west on the Lake Cushman road, past Lake Cushman State Park, turning left at a three-way junction onto Road 24. Follow the road along the shores of Lake Cushman into Olympic National Park to the Staircase Campground and Ranger Station at the end of the road.

Cross the concrete bridge over the North Fork of the Skokomish River in front of the ranger station and take the trail to the left (east) in front of the park service buildings.

The path starts out across a meadow beneath gnarled moss-draped maples along the river, passes a short abandoned miner's tunnel, and then contours between a steep cliff and the river. T'was here Staircase earned its name.

As photographer Ira Spring recalls (Bob and Ira Spring took the pictures in this book), at one time the only way to get up the river beyond the cliff was to climb a steep trail "staircase" over the top of the rock bluff, for there was no trail around it.

Today's trail was blasted out of the base of the cliff and signs of the old "staircase" have long been overgrown in this almost rain-forest corner of the park.

The trail ends on an abandoned road in a short mile, crosses Road 2451, and continues down another short unnumbered road to the path again. The trail here follows the shore of Lake Cushman another mile before turning uphill away from the lake.

Overhanging rock on the Staircase Loop trail

 2 Staircase Loop

Features: waterfalls and great trees
One way: 2-mile loop
Elevation gain: slight
Difficulty: moderate
Open: spring to fall
Maps: Green Trails 167; Custom Correct, Skokomish/Cushman

Hike along a staircase of spectacular rapids through moss-draped groves of maples and alders, cedars and Douglas firs.

To find the trail, drive west from Hoodsport on US Highway 101 on the Lake Cushman road, past Lake Cushman State Park. At a three-way junction with Road 24, turn left along the shores of Lake Cushman into Olympic National Park and the Staircase Ranger Station and Campground at the end of the road.

(Ignore the trail uphill from the ranger station that beckons many to Wagonwheel Lake. It's a steep, 3-mile grind.)

From the ranger station parking area, cross the concrete bridge over the North Fork of the Skokomish River following a well-worn path to the right (west) into lush forest. In ¼ mile or so, take a marked spur trail left to the base of an 800-year-old western red cedar 14 feet in diameter and 43 feet around. One of the largest in the park. Listen and watch here for pileated wood-peckers as they feed up and down the trees.)

Returning to the main path, continue above the turbulent staircase rapids with its noisy small falls and occasional clear pools. Some credit the steplike rapids for the area's name, but it was an actual mountain staircaselike trail over a lava bluff (see hike 1, Shady Lane) that truly gave the area its name.

You can either turn right and cross a metal bridge in a short mile or continue straight ahead on an interesting trail along the border of an area burned by fire in 1985. In ½ mile or so this sec-tion of trail, with close-up views of the burn and its continued slow recovery, passes a well-used camping spot on the river where an earlier bridge washed away many years ago. The forest fire started from a campfire here. The path climbs away from the river beyond this point, so turn back here.

If you cross today's metal bridge, turn right onto a road-now-trail to return to the parking area. (The trail to the left was once a road that led to Camp Pleasant, in about 7 miles.) As you re-turn, note the heavy erosion caused by a single flood in Slate Creek and also how slowly and how long it takes nature to defeat man's road-building efforts.

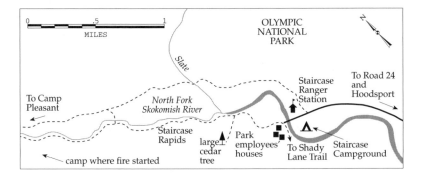

 Lena Lake

Features: forest, lake, and an earthquake's work
One way: 3½ miles
Elevation gain: 1,900 feet
Difficulty: moderate to steep
Open: summer
Maps: Green Trails 90; Custom Correct, Brothers/Anderson

A wonderful trail, truly. Steep but still one of the most popular in the Northwest. Be sure, though, as you hike here to note the great violence that caused it all.

From US Highway 101, turn west onto Road 25 about 2 miles north of Eldon, about a mile beyond the Hamma Hamma River bridge. Find a large trail parking area on the right in 8 miles.

The path starts out in an area logged at the turn of the century (views here over the valley) before climbing into old forest of cedar, Douglas fir, and hemlock. Lovely groves about halfway with mossy boulders, great cliffs, and overhanging bluffs.

The signs of earthquake violence begin at the bridge that in midsummer crosses a stream of boulders. (You can hear water flowing beneath the rocks.)

Only recently have scientists linked the buried stream and tree stubs in Lena Lake with earthquakes that shook Puget Sound beginning some 1,700 years ago.

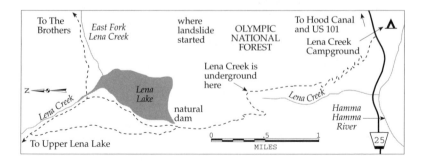

Camping on bluff above Lena Lake

Rock avalanches sparked by the quakes, studies showed, blocked streams and produced small lakes in which trees died in several places in the Olympics. Tree rings on submerged snags in Lena Lake fixed the event there at about 1,300 years ago. Similar quakes lifted shorelines more than twenty feet along Puget Sound, activated landslides in many areas, and triggered tsunamis that deposited sheets of sand in shallow bays around Puget Sound.

The trail drops to camp spots at the far end of the lake. Spur trails lead to Upper Lena Lake and toward The Brothers.

 4 Dose Forks

Features: great trees, swift river, rhododendrons
One way: 1½–2 miles
Elevation gain: 400–500 feet
Difficulty: moderate
Open: early summer to fall
Maps: Green Trails 168; Custom Correct, Gray Wolf/Dosewallips

Hike to a grove of tired and tumbling ancient trees and then through rhododendrons to a high old log bridge fitted together like jackstraws high above a gorge.

To find the trail drive north of Dosewallips State Park on US

Historic Dose Fork Shelter before it was removed by the Park Service

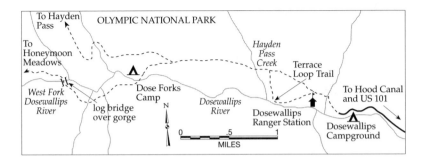

Highway 101, cross the Dosewallips River and turn west on the Dosewallips River road, driving 15 miles to the end of the road. And be warned: The last mile or so that climbs alongside Dosewallips Falls is very steep and narrow. Not for trailers or big campers.

The trail starts beyond the Dosewallips Campground from a parking lot below the ranger station.

The path climbs away from the river and passes the first entrance to a 1-mile Terrace Loop trail that winds through forest to a bench high above the river. (The second entrance—or exit—on the loop leads to a bench above river pools visited often by deer and elk.)

The main path continues above and away from the river until dropping down to a wood-truss bridge. Take time here before crossing the bridge to walk up the river through the primitive Dose Forks Camp. Note the great old trees that have already fallen there to winds and rot, and then walk to a small picnic and camp spot on a pool beside the river.

If you have the time, return to the trail and cross the bridge and walk on, first above the river and then through rhododendron gardens, to the log bridge in another long ¾ mile. (Rhododendrons here bloom as spring makes its way up into the mountains—here in late May and early June.)

The jackstraw bridge, a piece of woodsman's art, levered, cantilevered, and counter-levered once again with now-gray logs, spans the West Fork Dosewallips River as it plunges through a narrow gorge to meet the main river. Rest here on mossy logs and wonder about the skill it took to weave and interweave those logs all, no doubt, cut near the site.

5 | Falls View

Features: waterfall, rhododendrons, a river too
One way: ¾ mile
Elevation gain: about 200 feet
Difficulty: moderate to steep
Open: early spring to late fall
Maps: Olympic National Forest; Olympic National Park

A quick and easy walk leads to a view of a waterfall, while a stiff climb into and out of a canyon yields rhododendrons, tumbling rapids, rich forest, and shoulder-high ferns.

Find all of the trails here in Falls View Campground on US Highway 101 about 4 miles south of Quilcene. Turn left as you enter the campground and then right on a loop road to a signed trail and parking area.

Start with the waterfalls. A level trail of 50 yards or less strolls to the right from the campground parking area through chest-high salal and evergreen huckleberry to a view down on a waterfall that plunges 100 feet from an unnamed stream over a canyon wall into the Big Quilcene River. A delicate veil during late summer but a torrent during high water.

The trip into the canyon, however, with its blossoming rhododendrons in the spring and tumbling rapids and river all the time, is a different story. No stroll here. It's down, down, down going in and climb, climb, climb coming out.

Find this trail to the left of the parking area. It switchbacks through rhododendrons to the river, turns left across a creek just before reaching the river, and then wanders upstream, climbing

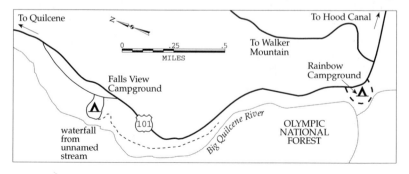

Unnamed waterfall seen from Falls View Campground

as the river climbs, to wherever it is you want to stop. Acres of ferns, moss-draped maples, big cottonwoods. Noisy river. With fisherman paths occasionally to pools on the river's edge.

The trail climbs up and inland toward the end with no real purpose in mind.

(Note: From Rainbow Campground, about a mile south of Falls View on US Highway 101, a short hike also leads to the river with a glimpse of a waterfall through trees to the left en route. The path ends steeply at the river.)

6 Mount Zion

Features: vistas, vistas, vistas
One way: 1¾ miles
Elevation gain: 1,300 feet
Difficulty: steep to steeper
Open: summer
Maps: Green Trails 136; Custom Correct, Buckhorn

On a clear day here you can almost see forever:

From Vancouver, British Columbia, to the north to Mount Adams to the south. With Port Angeles, Victoria, the Space Needle, all of the Cascades, Glacier Peak, and Mount Rainier, the Strait of Juan de Fuca, the San Juan Islands, Hood Canal— and everything in between.

Drive north out of Quilcene on US Highway 101 for 2 miles, turning left on County Road 30, the first major side road. At the T-junction at Lords Lake, take Road 28 left to Bon Jon Pass,

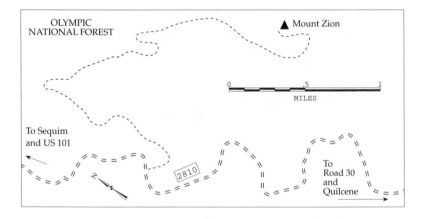

View from old lookout site on Mount Zion

avoiding all tempting spurs left in the next 2 miles. At the pass, bear right on Road 2810, watching for a trail sign on the right in another 2 miles. Don't be tempted to take another way out. Roads are almost impossible to follow. Return the way you came.

The trail starts up sharply, winds through rhododendrons, and continues steeply to the rocky site of the former lookout on Mount Zion. Places to rest here and enjoy the splendor of the scene. Bring water—and your lunch—before making your way back down.

And, oh yes, bring a forest or road map to help you identify all that you see from cities there to mountains far, far beyond.

A geography lesson here if nothing else. And a geology lesson too if you're into the history of rocks.

Container ship and Point Wilson Lighthouse

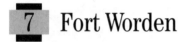 Fort Worden

Features: beaches, forest, history, vistas
One way: 1 mile plus
Elevation gain: none to 100 feet
Difficulty: easy to moderate
Open: all year
Map: Fort Worden State Park map

Stroll beaches here with sea birds, seals, and sea lions. Hike into a forest with the season's flowers, sweeping vistas, and hidden memories of war.

Find all of these in Fort Worden State Park in the northeastern corner of Port Townsend on the Strait of Juan de Fuca and Admiralty Inlet. Follow street signs through town.

Beach hikes or strolls stretch both south and west from Point Wilson and its lighthouse where the strait and inlet meet.

A sand beach stretches south of the lighthouse point with birds—including puffins, sometimes—feeding in the protected cove or in the faster water of the inlet's tidal stream. This beach stretches beyond the park wharf with its Marine Science Center to the southern boundary of the park.

West along the north shore of the strait, an unmarked beach extends from the lighthouse point to the western border of the park. The hiking on this beach is best at low tide. Some rocks midway can be covered with water at high tide.

Watch here even in the roughest weather for gulls of several sorts, cormorants, harlequin ducks, scoters, buffleheads—to barely start a list.

Seals are likely to pop up to watch you along either of these shores. Sea lions spend most of their time here fishing off Point Wilson at the lighthouse in the fast water during changing tides.

Inland trails along the top of the bluff start in the campground and end in meadows at the western boundary of the park. Find the trail from the campground uphill from the first site on the north loop camp. It's signed.

The path climbs sharply to the top of the bluff and then wends to the right past several abandoned coast artillery gun emplacements, installed to protect the entrance to the sound but never used in war and now stripped of guns. Views here out over the strait at passing freighters and dim outlines of the San Juans and Vancouver Island.

For details on other trails that loop through the area, get a map from the park office.

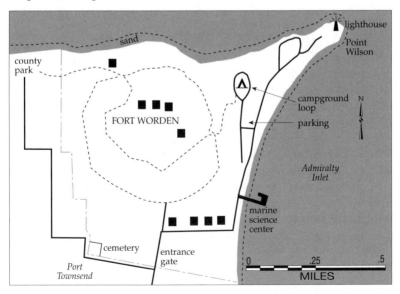

Footbridge over Dungeness River

8 Dungeness River

Features: lush forest, fast river
One way: 1 mile plus
Elevation gain: about 200 feet
Difficulty: easy
Open: early spring to fall
Maps: Green Trails 136; Custom Correct, Buckhorn Wilderness

No hike here: a stroll. Through an ancient forest beside a tumbling river and then into an old-but-younger forest and a still-tumbling river.

Turn south off US Highway 101 onto Louella Road across from Sequim Bay State Park (about 4 miles southeast of Sequim).

Turn left at an intersection in about a mile and follow the county road into the national forest and Road 28. From Road 28, turn left onto Road 2860, following it to the trailhead on the Dungeness River. About 18 miles from US Highway 101.

A short switchback leads from a trailhead parking area to a bench above the river where giant trees seem bent in a slugging match to see which giants will win the battle for forest sunlight here. Some great giants already lie defeated on the ground while others stand broken, still waiting to fall. Only the old cedars here seem unscathed by the battle so far.

And where the sun breaks through the old towering trees, clumps of new conifers, rhododendrons, seedlings on top of mossy nurse logs, and flowers on the forest floor argue over every new little spot of light.

At the start of the trail, all sorts of paths wind above the river with dozens of places to pause and soak up the scene.

In a mile, before crossing a bridge to the left over Royal Creek, take time to examine the huge moss- and fern-covered boulders that have fallen into Royal Creek straight ahead. This trail climbs on to Royal Basin in 6 more miles.

Returning, cross the bridge to the Buckhorn Wilderness and a path that climbs first away from the main river and then back again to soggy spots with old log bridges now and then.

Turn back whenever the spirit moves you. An unmarked salt lick in less than 1 mile. Watch for lots of animal tracks. Camp Handy shelter in another 2½ miles.

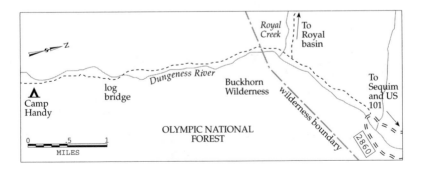

 9 Dungeness Spit

Features: beaches and birds
One way: 2 miles and more
Elevation gain: none
Difficulty: easy
Open: all year
Map: any Washington state highway map

You can look out at the spit from bluffs and roads all along the shoreline here. But to truly savor the sudden wildness of this National Wildlife Refuge with its sea birds and shorebirds, you must walk its shores and climb its piles of driftwood.

From US Highway 101 in Sequim, drive north out of town on the road to the town of Dungeness, turning left at the old landmark schoolhouse and crossing the Dungeness River before the road enters the community. Beyond the bridge, follow all roads closest to the shore until you reach the entrance to Dungeness Recreation Area. Turn right and drive past a county campground to a large parking lot overlooking the spit. A Golden Eagle card or $2 voluntary fee are suggested.

A signed trail leads first through trees to an overlook and then down to the beach.

There are no formal trails on the spit. The beaches to the right face a cove protected by the spit. The beach to the left, more exposed to wind and waves, faces the Strait of Juan de Fuca. Walk out one side and return the other. No camping, beach fires, or bicycles are permitted in the wildlife refuge.

You'll meet lots of hikers at the start of any hike here, but a

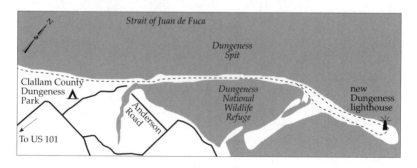

walk of 2 miles will bring you solitude. And don't be deluded by the apparent distance to the lighthouse. It's about 7 miles.

(The beach beyond the lighthouse is closed as a seal pupping area. The large area south of the spit and lighthouse is closed to protect nesting birds.)

Bird life here varies with the season. During the spring and fall, you'll find migrating plovers, sandpipers, dunlins, and sanderlings. In the winter, whistling swans and brants with loons, grebes, scaups. All year, ducks and gulls of many kinds.

(Hikers are asked to not disturb feeding birds. Such interruptions prevent migrating birds from acquiring the food they need.)

Bring your telescope or binoculars. A bird book, for certain. Lunch. A blanket, maybe, to stave off the constant wind. And lots and lots of patience. And leave no trash. Please!

Driftwood on Dungeness Spit

 10 Deer Park

Features: spectacles of alpine flowers, views
One way: up to 2 miles
Elevation gain: up to 200 feet
Difficulty: moderate to steep
Open: midsummer
Maps: Green Trails 135–136; Custom Correct, Gray Wolf/
   Dosewallips

Three hikes here out of many. All through alpine meadows with spectacular views.

From US Highway 101—about 4 miles east of Port Angeles, 11 miles west of Sequim, and just east of the big curve that drops into a valley—turn south on a signed road and drive to the Deer Park Campground in 17 miles.

Green Mountain: Take the Grand Ridge trail downhill from the ranger's house (on a spur road before you reach the campground) and hike 2 miles to a high saddle beyond Green Mountain.

The trail drops at first and then climbs to a ridge with flowers and trees. After skirting Green Mountain, the path climbs to an alpine saddle with views into Olympic National Park and over the Strait of Juan de Fuca.

Blue Mountain: Drive a steep road uphill, north of the campground, to a point below the mountain top and the one-

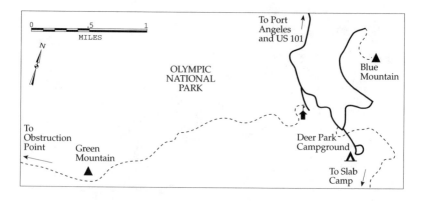

Three deer at Deer Park Campground

time site of a lookout (6,007 feet). Walk to the top for views down on Port Angeles, across the strait to Victoria, out at the San Juan Islands and Mount Baker, and around to mountain ridges in the park.

Follow only well-marked paths here to note and preserve the fragile flowers clinging to the rocks: Start with wild onions. Sedum. Phlox. Saxifrages. Even violets.

Slab Camp Trail: Hike along an alpine ridge on a trail that starts in a meadow off the west corner of the campground and promptly climbs to open views into the park. Flower-decorated rock outcrops here, alpine trees, vistas, even deer.

At about a mile the trail starts down, again on open slopes. Turn back before the trail drops into forest. Slab Camp in 5 miles.

Meadow on Obstruction Point

11 Obstruction Point

Features: grand meadows, distant views
One way: 2 miles plus
Elevation gain: 300 feet
Difficulty: moderate to steep
Open: midsummer
Maps: Green Trails 135; Custom Correct, Gray Wolf/Dosewallips

Cross rolling tundra hills that dwarf everything you see. With only marmots, deer perhaps, and clumps of wind-bent trees to give perspective to the scene.

From US Highway 101 in Port Angeles, follow signs to Hurricane Ridge, turning downhill to the left on the Obstruction

Point road about 0.25 mile before the paved road reaches the Hurricane Ridge Visitor Center.

The gravel road here is the most spectacular and exciting in Olympic National Park, winding in places along ridge tops with vistas both right and left. Find the trailhead off the parking area at the end of the road in 7.8 miles.

The trail drops to the south away from the parking area and climbs to the top of a rolling ridge with a small knoblike viewing point. From the ridge, views into the park off both sides of the trail. Even Mount Olympus, the highest of many peaks to the west.

In about ½ mile, across what seems like endless tundra, the path drops down some steps around a stream head and then starts a steep climb to a point where the trail begins its drop to Grand and Moose lakes in Grand Valley. Stop here at the highest point. More vistas still.

A warning, though: These inviting, peaceful-looking slopes can be dangerous. There is no place to seek refuge here from the biting, chilling winds that sometimes sweep these ridges even in midsummer. The winds have proven fatal to a few hikers caught in the open here. So watch the weather. Be conscious of the wind. And be prepared to abandon plans.

And yes, whistle at marmots as you start your walk, along the way, and as you return. They seem to appreciate the chatter.

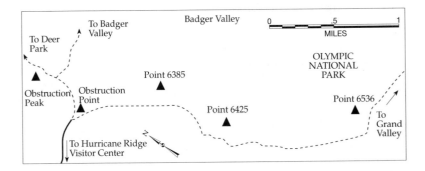

 Hurricane Meadows

Features: alpine forest, meadows, views
One way: 1 mile, less or longer
Elevation gain: 200 feet or less
Difficulty: moderate to steep
Open: summer
Map: Hurricane Ridge nature trail map (Park Service)

More people than flowers here on weekends. But still a fine sample of alpine ridges and alpine meadows in the Olympic Mountains.

From Port Angeles, turn south of US Highway 101 and follow signs to the Hurricane Ridge Visitor Center in 17 miles.

Find a host of trails here on the north side of the road that cross meadows, wind into alpine forest, and ascend to viewpoints.

For a sample of the best, take a trail marked Klahhane Ridge uphill at the east end of the parking lot. The path climbs steadily across meadows and through trees to a junction with the Klahhane Ridge trail.

(Take time here to walk to your right out the ridge as far as you'd like. Constant airplane views here both north over the Strait of Juan de Fuca and south into the national park over the road leading to Hurricane Ridge. The path continues around Mount Angeles to the Heart of the Hills Campground in a long 7 miles.)

To remain near the Hurricane Ridge complex, bear left at the junction and climb on to Sunrise Point, a popular viewing point.

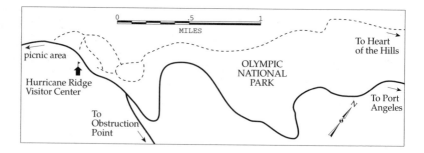

From there return on the High Ridge and Cirque Rim trails (or any other of several paths) to the parking lot again.

Constant views here through trees and over meadows to the south and out over Port Angeles and the Strait of Juan de Fuca to the north.

Alpine flowers highlight any walk here when the meadows bloom in late summer. But don't pick them, please. Look at them, most certainly. Take pictures of them too. But leave them undisturbed so others can see them too.

And take your pictures from the trail. The soil here is very fragile, as you'll note everywhere along these upthrust ridges of rock. Step on a flower and it's most certainly dead.

Watch for marmots and deer here in addition to the ubiquitous chipmunks.

Hurricane Ridge Lodge and Mount Carrie from meadow trail

Hurricane Hill trail

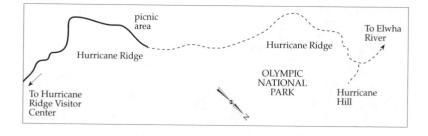

13 Hurricane Hill

Features: grand vistas, flowers too
One way: 1½ miles
Elevation gain: about 700 feet
Difficulty: moderate to steep
Open: midsummer
Maps: Green Trails 134; Custom Correct, Hurricane Ridge

Hike to a former lookout site for the best of all vistas here. Busy often but seldom overrun.

From Port Angeles, turn south off US Highway 101 and follow signs into Olympic National Park and on to the visitor center at Hurricane Ridge in 17 miles.

Find the trailhead beyond the visitor center off the end of a paved loop beyond a picnic area in about 1.3 miles.

The trail, actually a narrow road that once ran uphill to a former lookout, proceeds fairly level about the first ½ mile before beginning its persistent climb to a grassy ridge and site of the former lookout.

Flower fields, here as elsewhere along Hurricane Ridge, as the path climbs steadily for about ¾ mile and then switchbacks to the small meadow at the top.

Short walks up the lookout knoll or to edges of the ridge lead to vistas. A trail to the right leads to views over the Strait of Juan de Fuca. A trail left, which drops eventually to the Elwha Ranger Station in 6 miles, affords views both north and south.

Views of everything from the knoll, of course. Of all the ranges to the south, Port Angeles, Vancouver Island, Victoria, the San Juan Islands, Mount Baker, and the Cascade Range.

Take a lunch. No water at the top. And carry a jacket too. The wind here can be chilly even on a sunny day. And, please, don't hurry. Take time to soak up everything you see. From the close-up flowers to mountains far away.

Marymere Falls

 Marymere Falls

Features: a waterfall, forest
One way: 1 mile
Elevation gain: 400 feet
Difficulty: moderate to steep
Open: often year-round
Maps: Green Trails 101; Lake Crescent hike map (Park Service)

Walk an easy trail through a lush forest along a creek before climbing steep stairs to a slender, shaded 90-foot waterfall.

Drive west of Port Angeles on US Highway 101 into Olympic

National Park. On the south side of Lake Crescent, turn right at the exit to the Storm King Ranger Station. Find the trail in front of the ranger station.

The path drops beneath Highway 101 and crosses a meadow before entering a dark, dense forest of cedar, hemlock, and Douglas fir. Note the rotting nurse stumps here straddled by firs now supported on stilts. Note too the new clusters of fir growing in forest places now open to the sun. Unmarked spur trails lead right to grand groves of old trees growing along the creek.

In about ¼ mile, pass a trail (on the left) that climbs steeply on Mount Storm King to viewpoints over Lake Crescent. (Signs warn inexperienced hikers there of climbing dangers as the trail nears the summit.)

On the waterfall trail, in ¾ mile turn right, away from the Barnes Creek trail that goes on to Happy Ridge, and cross a log bridge to big maples cloaked with moss.

Beyond the bridge, take a junction to the left up wooden steps for the steepest, quickest, and fullest views of the falls. Find a torrent here that does not shout but whispers as a formal lady should. From a viewing platform at the top, return down a spur that turns away from the falls and loops back down to the trail.

Note as you return how far the noise of logging trucks on Highway 101 reaches into the forest before finally being silenced by the trees and waterfall.

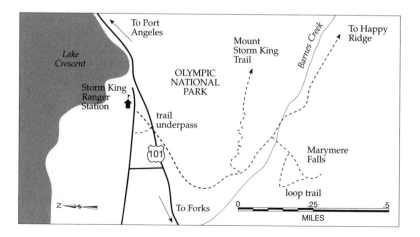

One of two tunnels along old Spruce Railroad

15 Spruce Railroad Trail

Features: lake, vistas, tunnels, history
One way: 1–4 miles
Elevation gain: moderate to level
Difficulty: easy
Open: year-round
Maps: Green Trails 101; Custom Correct, Lake Crescent/Happy
   Lake

There are at least three ways to walk the shoreline of Lake Crescent, enjoy the scenery, and see two collapsed railroad tunnels along the way.

A 1¼-mile walk leads to one tunnel south of the Log Cabin Resort at East Beach on the north end of Lake Crescent in Olympic National Park. A walk of about a mile leads to another tunnel on a trail at the end of the North Shore Road beyond Fairholm Campground. And a 4-mile walk from one trailhead to the other leads past both tunnels if you can arrange for a ride at one end or the other.

To reach the trail at East Beach on the north end of the lake, turn north off US Highway 101 at the top of the ridge between Lake Sutherland and Lake Crescent onto the East Beach Road.

Just beyond the Log Cabin Resort at the far end of the lake, turn left on Road 3079 (signed Spruce Railroad Trail) and follow it to the end. Park on the left side of the road just beyond a bridge, finding the trail uphill across from the signed parking area. (Private property borders both sides of the parking area.)

The path here climbs to the old railroad bed well above the lake and remains in forest until it drops to the lake at Devil Point.

Buried timbers in the forest above the trail mark the north entrance of one tunnel as the trail starts to drop around the point. Find the other end of the tunnel, filled with gravel and rock, behind a fence well above the shore beyond the point.

Most interesting on this trail are the basalt cliffs, a bridged cove, and views over Lake Crescent at the mountains.

Find the Fairholm end of the trail 5 miles from Highway 101 at the end of the North Shore Road along Lake Crescent beyond Fairholm Campground. Turn off Highway 101 at the west end of Lake Crescent at the Fairholm Campground sign.

The path starts beside a huge Douglas fir, climbs immediately to the railroad right-of-way, and then drops gradually along the base of cliffs to the shore and the short, open second tunnel through a basalt point of rock. Fallen rock and timbers signal the dangers here.

Look but don't explore and then follow the main trail along the shoreline around the point to the barely visible exit above the trail, to the left, at the top of blasted rock debris.

The trail between the two tunnels remains mainly in trees with only occasional views out.

And why all the fuss about the tunnels here? They are all that's left of a million-dollar government railroad, built in World War II but never used, to get spruce timber from the forest.

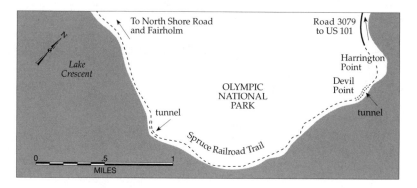

 Sol Duc Falls

Features: forest, waterfall
One way: 1-, 2¼-, and 4-mile loops
Elevation gain: slight
Difficulty: moderate
Open: summer
Maps: Green Trails 133; Custom Correct, Seven Lakes/Hoh

The beauty of this waterfall? All the words here must be yours. The grandeur of the plants? Yours too. The trails? Again, the words are yours to find. The only thing said here is that it's a place you should not miss.

To find this jewel—you can start by saying that, at least—turn left from US Highway 101 at the top of the ridge 1.9 miles west of Lake Crescent onto the Sol Duc Road.

For the shortest hike to the falls, drive to a trailhead at the end of the road in 13.8 miles. For two longer hikes where others must pick you up, start (or end) at Sol Duc Campground in 12.2 miles or the hot-springs resort in 11.8 miles.

From the end of the road, the trail passes through an ancient forest displaying every phase of growth. In one place trees have just begun to argue over which large middle-aged trees will survive to be giants. In another, some failed giants already lie sprawled on the forest floor, having lost their fight. And in other places, in occasional patches of sunlight, new seedling trees continue childish arguments over sharing their sunlight and space.

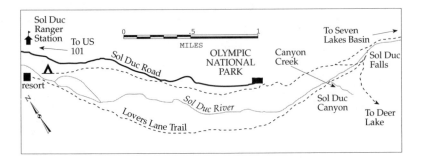

At the end of a mile the path turns downhill toward the river, passing below a classic-but-rebuilt shelter, to a bridge and the first views of the falls. Across the bridge turn left to a viewing platform with places to sit, rest, watch, and listen to the falls.

And be sure to look beyond what man has built here. Be sure to note the guardian growth of prickly devil's club to the right of the bridge, the polished channels in the rock on the far side (wonder how long it took to etch the bowls you see below the wooden viewing deck), and the four-fingered plumes of water that etch new rock channels still.

Sol Duc Falls

Return one of three ways here:

(1) The way you came, listening this time to all of the languages you'll hear spoken by foreign visitors hiking here.

(2) Remain on the far side of the river and follow the Lovers Lane trail back 3 miles to the resort on an easy water-grade trail that weaves into forest away from the river at times and then back to mossy, open places on the stream. (Completing a 4-mile trip designed for lovers for sure.)

(3) Walk back toward the road on the main trail, turning left just short of the parking lot to a trail that wanders back to the Sol Duc Campground in 1½ miles. No highway this. Rather, a path that lets you touch and feel the grandeur of a forest here.

Shi Shi Beach

17   Shi Shi Beach

Features: reefs, Pacific Ocean beaches
One way: 2 miles
Elevation gain: slight
Difficulty: easy to moderate
Open: year-round
Maps: Green Trails 98S; Custom Correct, North Olympic Coast

A great sweeping beach on the shore of the Pacific Ocean capped with rugged reefs and headlands.

Check with Olympic National Park officials in Port Angeles before attempting any trip here. In 1994, the 2-mile access trail

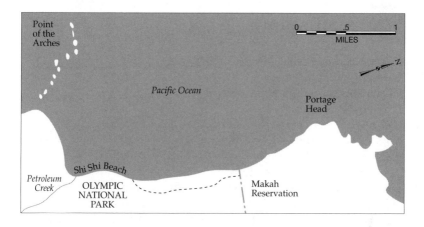

south of Neah Bay to the national park boundary across part of
the Makah Reservation was closed to public entry as the park
and Makah Tribe continued negotiating access questions.

At the park/reservation boundary, an unmarked path drops
down to a sand beach that sweeps south 3 miles to Point of the
Arches, one of the most dramatic collection of sea stacks, tide
pools, and hidden coves on any public section of beach along the
Pacific Ocean coast.

To the north a short hike leads to other rock spires, small
coves, and headlands.

It's best to explore all headlands here at low tides. So carry a
tide book and a map that identifies tidal danger spots. Carry
guide books too that identify tidal creatures and plants. And
leave all tide-pool life where you find it. Even a generous sea
cannot keep up with the unthinking curiosity of man.

And yes, respect the Makah ownership of all the land north
of the park, which includes all of the beaches on Makah Bay. The
Makahs respect and cherish all of these lands. The rest of us
should do so too.

 Cape Alava

Features: headlands, beach, history
One way: 3 miles or more
Elevation gain: about 100 feet
Difficulty: easy
Open: year-round
Maps: Green Trails 130S; Custom Correct, North Olympic Coast

A longer hike here than most in this book, but one of the most interesting. For it crosses a lush environment lived in by Native Americans for 2,000 years at least and then by immigrant farmers who tried to settle here at the turn of the century.

At the westernmost point of the lower continental United States.

Drive west from Clallam Bay on Highway 112, turn south in about 4 miles onto a county road, and drive 21 miles to the Ozette Ranger Station on Lake Ozette in Olympic National Park.

Find the trail across the Ozette River (behind a kiosk to the left of the parking area). At a T-junction in about ¼ mile, turn right onto the Cape Alava Trail. Follow a boardwalk all the way to the beach. (The planked path can be extremely slippery when wet. Lug soles are not recommended.)

Beyond the junction, the path passes through forest about a mile before climbing slightly to an open area, once a meadow, farmed within this century by two brothers who hauled everything including a gas-powered sawmill over the trail from Clallam Bay.

Beyond a clearing, still called Ahlstroms Prairie, the path returns to forest on a wooden path with minor ups and down to a point on the ocean facing Ozette Island.

Ozette Indians lived along this beautiful section of coast for at least twenty centuries before moving early in this century to Makah Bay so their children could attend school.

Hike north along the beach about ¾ mile to Tskawahyah (Cannonball) Island surrounded by large cannonball concretions eroded from the island cliffs over millions of years. Reach the island and its cannonballs at low tide. Don't plan to carry any home. They weigh hundreds of pounds.

If you walk the beach here at low tide, note the wandering,

Sailboat (left) *and Killer whale* (right) *petroglyphs at Wedding Rocks*

winding pathways in the tideland rocks. The people who once lived here cleared them to confuse attacking enemies and wreck their war canoes and also to permit the landing of the huge gray whales hunters often killed offshore.

Also, hike south along the beach a mile from the trailhead to a small headland called Wedding Rocks to view petroglyphs carved in boulders near the shore.

Watch for sea otters and eagles and perhaps blowing whales far offshore. Camp and picnic spots. (Special national park permits are required for camping here.)

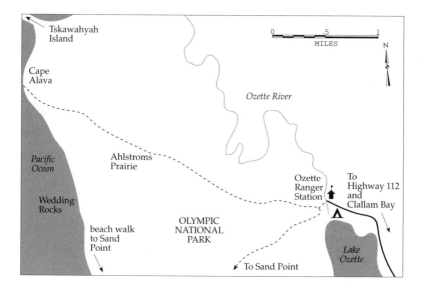

19   Sand Point

Features: a rock-spire point, beaches, vistas
One way: 2¾ miles or more
Elevation gain: slight
Difficulty: easy
Open: year-round
Maps: Green Trails 130S; Custom Correct, North Olympic Coast

Walk an up-and-down boardwalk trail through dense salal and a beach forest of Sitka spruce to a green spire at the end of a sand spit.

Drive west from Clallam Bay on Highway 112, turn south in about 4 miles onto a county road, and drive 21 miles to Lake Ozette and the Ozette Ranger Station in Olympic National Park.

Find the trail across the Ozette River (behind a kiosk to the left of the parking area). Turn left onto the Sand Point trail at a T-junction in about ¼ mile. Follow the boardwalk all the way to the beach. (The planked path can be extremely slippery when wet. Lug soles are not recommended.)

Ferns, evergreen huckleberry, occasional trees, and bursts of red-berried bunchberry crowd the path. But salal—the ubiquitous evergreen bush with the fuzzy, tasty berry—dominates this lowland forest, pushing and shoving its way into every open place.

The sound of the ocean surf announces its presence as the planked path nears the ocean where weathered Sitka spruce crowd out the light and sword ferns claim the ground.

Explore two beaches at the point. The first, a protected bay north of the point sheltered from dominant southwest winds. Here look for sea otters, listen for oystercatchers, watch cormo-

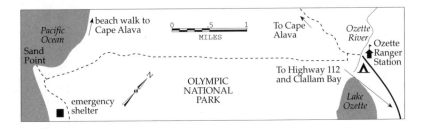

rants and buffleheads dive and dive and dive again. And in the distance sometimes see spouting whales and twisting V's of geese and brant and, with great good luck, along the shore, peregrine falcons. Deer outclass raccoons and occasional bears here in stealing food from backpacks suspended in trees. The deer have learned to stand up on their hind legs to slash the bottom of the highest pack with their hooves.

On the south side of the point, the rolling ocean and wind command everything. Waves burst over rocks and string white foam toward the shore. Gulls pose in clusters against the wind on spits of sand. And at low tide, piles of drifted sea debris and kelp lie tangled everywhere.

And the sand point? A spur of rock actually. Blanketed with grass. Watch for deer grazing atop the point as you climb sharp switchbacks to the top. A place to pose, as others do, and wave your accomplishment. Sometimes deer may share the point even as you wave.

National park permits are required for overnight camping anywhere on these beaches.

Beach south of Sand Point

20   Slough and James Pond Trails

Features: forest, pond
One way: up to about 1¼ miles
Elevation gain: none
Difficulty: easy
Open: year-round
Maps: Green Trails 163S; Custom Correct, South Olympic Coast

Two respites here, truly. First a short trail to a restful pond that begs to be waited near and watched. Then a wander through lush forest above a quiet slough.

From US Highway 101, turn west about 4 miles north of Forks onto the road to La Push. In 8 miles bear right on a road to Mora and Rialto Beach. Find both trails near the ranger station at Mora Campground in another 2.8 miles.

Start the ⅓-mile loop trail to James Pond west of the Olympic National Park Ranger Station. The path crosses the main road and then loops through rich, quiet forest to the edge of the pond and a view-log jutting from the shore. Along the trail see skunk cabbages and trilliums in the spring. And the colors of vine maples in the fall.

If you're quiet approaching the pond, who knows what you may see? A muskrat perhaps. Deer or elk. A startled frog. Water birds for sure. With luck, a gangly great blue heron landing high in some tree and walking along a branch to a hidden nest. (Until you've seen one, you have a right to laugh. Such a long-legged bird perched high on a limb? Impossible!)

Find the Slough Trail east of the ranger station entrance road beyond the parking lot. This path wends about 1 mile through a rich forest of hemlock and Sitka spruce. Note the fluted hemlocks common near the coast.

Trilliums, the yellow cones of spruce and the tiny cones of hemlock, fat yellow salmonberries, ferns of several sorts, and shy Oregon oxalis start the plant show here in early spring.

A signed spur trail leads to the Quillayute River about two-thirds of the way. The trail ends across from the national park entrance sign on the main entrance road. Walk back the way you came.

James Pond

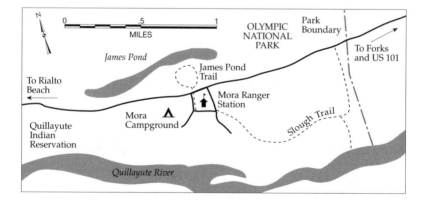

Hole-in-the-Wall

21 Hole-in-the-Wall

Features: exciting beach, tunnel in rock
One way: 1½ miles
Elevation gain: none
Difficulty: moderate
Open: during low tides, year-round
Maps: Green Trail 130S; Custom Correct, South Olympic Coast

Rialto Beach with its big waves and pounding surf—only steps away from your car—has to be the main course served here. But a hole in the wall etched by the ocean in a small headland cliff is a relish not to be missed.

(Plan your trip during a low-tide period. Tide tables are usually posted at the Olympic National Park Ranger Station at Mora Campground and on the rest-room notice board at Rialto Beach.)

From US Highway 101, turn west about 4 miles north of Forks onto the road to La Push. In 8 miles bear right, driving to the end of the road at Rialto Beach.

From the parking area, follow a path beyond the rest room to the beach. (Look north here to see the "hole" in the cluster of shore-bound sea stacks about 1½ miles away.)

Walk north about a mile up the beach to Ellen Creek, crossing the creek over scrambles of driftwood and makeshift slab bridges, or barefoot through the stream if it is low enough or the tide is out.

Or, if pirouettes and arabesques atop slippery logs are not among your hiking skills, simply turn back and enjoy all of the other wonders here.

Beyond the creek, continue up the beach ½ mile or so, crossing behind two sea stacks to a third with its rock tunnel, hole-in-the-wall view back toward La Push.

Admire the violence of the place, prowl the tide pools, and then return before the tide comes in.

Every stretch of this beach deserves, indeed, demands exploration. The constant deafening sound of exploding surf and rushing waves cannot be ignored. But the fresh footprints of birds and animals, monstrous drift logs tossed far up on the shore, the barren, battered, storm-stripped trees on the forest's edge, the picnic tables buried in gravel beneath picnic-area trees—all must be sought out and examined to appreciate the fullness of life and violence here.

And yes, if you're lucky you might—just might—find a glass ball on the sand—blown there all the way from Japan. Or see a whale spouting in the sea offshore. Or hear a seal applauding as you walk by. Or simply stand in awe as sunset colors flood the western sea and sky.

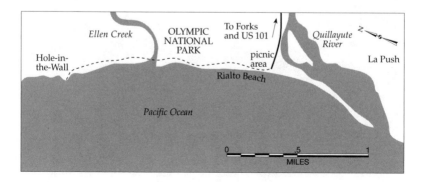

Driftwood at Second Beach

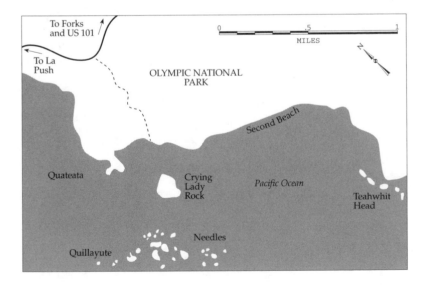

To Forks
and US 101

To La
Push

OLYMPIC NATIONAL
PARK

0   .5   1
MILES

N

Second Beach

Quateata

Crying
Lady
Rock

Pacific Ocean

Teahwhit
Head

Needles

Quillayute

22 Second Beach

Features: forest, beach, rock headlands
One way: ¾ mile and more
Elevation gain: about 200 feet
Difficulty: moderate to steep
Open: year-round
Maps: Green Trails 163S; Custom Correct, South Olympic Coast

Hike through inviting forest to one of the most spectacular and exciting beaches on this section of the coast.

From US Highway 101 about 4 miles north of Forks, turn west and follow signs about 14 miles toward La Push and the boundary of Olympic National Park. Find the trailhead parking lot on the left as the road drops down into La Push.

The path starts around a fenced water source for a nearby tribal salmon hatchery, and then climbs immediately into rich forest filled with grand old trees, snags, stumps, nurse logs, seedlings, and young trees: everything it takes to keep such a forest living forever.

Note the great variety of ways new trees find to grow here and the equal variety of ways old trees find to decay. The path here may be muddy in the winter.

In ½ mile the path starts down a long stretch of wooden steps and platforms to the scenic beach.

In addition to the sweeping beach, you'll find sea stacks here scattered offshore, a hole eroded in a headland to the right. And for history, far to the left, at the end of the beach, note the cliffs, spires, and rocks of Teahwhit Head, where a friendly Russian freighter during a gale in World War II was thrown into cliffs and rocks in the middle of the night. All but one of the Russian crew were saved by U.S. Coast Guardsmen who, working from the dangerous cliffs, threw lines to the stricken vessel foundering on its side in a raging surf, its lifeboats wrecked.

(Make no attempt to explore here. No trail over the headland or around the dangerous cliffs. And there is no debris left from the 1943 April Fools Day wreck.)

 Third Beach

Features: beaches, sea stacks
One way: 1½ miles
Elevation gain: 300 feet
Difficulty: moderate
Open: year-round
Maps: Green Trails 163S; Custom Correct, South Olympic Coast

Start here on a trail that leads first through forest to lovely Strawberry Bay and then over headlands and along other wilderness beaches to the Hoh River in 17 miles.

From US Highway 101 about 4 miles north of Forks, turn west and follow signs toward La Push and Olympic National Park. Find the trailhead on the left in about 12 miles from 101.

The path starts down an old logging road grown over with alder. The old road, however, shortly turns into a gravel trail that winds into a young forest growing amid stumps, fallen logs, and root fans of an old forest, passing finally into a forest ravaged by a storm where young trees again sprout from stumps and nurse logs amid vine maple, sword fern, and oxalis. In the last ¼ mile, the path drops to the beach along a creek.

On Strawberry Bay, the beach to the right ends against Teahwhit Head which cannot be rounded either by trail over the top or on the beach at low tide.

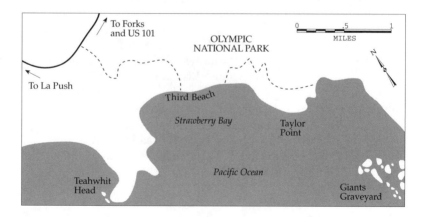

Waterfall on Taylor Head from Third Beach

The beach to the south ends against Taylor Point. A waterfall tumbles there from a cliff. A section of the south wilderness coast trail that ends at the Hoh River turns inland in less than ½ mile at a target-signed trail entrance. The first section of this path climbs 1¼ miles over Taylor Point to the next beach.

24 Hoh Nature Trails

Features: lush rain forest, huge trees
One way: 2 miles on 2 loops
Elevation gain: none
Difficulty: easy
Open: year-round
Maps: Green Trails 133; Custom Correct, Bogachiel Valley

Two trails here—and you should walk them both—spell out everything a Pacific Northwest "rain forest" means.

But do not—do not—rush over either of them or you will miss—truly miss—the essence of them both. For it's not what you see here but what you take time to feel and understand that really counts.

From Forks, on US Highway 101, drive south about 14 miles and then turn east on the Hoh Valley Road, driving 19 miles to the Hoh Visitor Center in Olympic National Park. Find both of these trails off a paved loop that starts in front of the visitor center.

Hall of Mosses Nature Trail: This ¾-mile loop winds through a picture-book example of moss-draped trees and lush undergrowth in a climax rain forest.

Frost-covered maple leaves

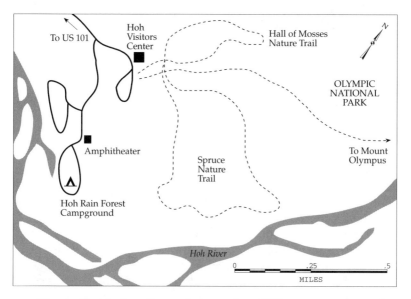

The path circles through towering Sitka spruce into the cathedral-like Hall of Mosses before returning to the paved loop.

Spruce Nature Trail: This 1½-mile loop off the main paved nature trail (keep right at the fork) leads away from crowds into stands of towering spruce and moss-draped groves of vine maples, eventually dropping to a flat near the Hoh River. No great marked vistas here. Only the quiet splendor of an ancient forest evolving constantly from life to decay. The special vistas are yours to find.

On both of these trails, take note: There are more than great trees here. There are shades of green beyond counting and changes in light and shade that add new magic to every place you walk. And there are shy elk that keep every patch of open meadow groomed like a park.

Morning here, even in the densest forest, is always different from afternoon with mists, fog, and sun adding their own changes to the scene. As good photographers always note.

And beyond the grandeur of the trees, note the smaller plants and flowers that dominate the open forest floor. They demand attention too. So you'll need a flower book.

Camping at the campground here will give you time to see all of these smaller things.

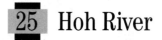 25 Hoh River

Features: river, forest, meadow
One way: 2 miles plus
Elevation gain: none
Difficulty: easy
Open: year-round
Maps: Green Trails 133; Custom Correct, Bogachiel Valley

A river, yes. One that sweeps and has swept its way back and forth across this valley for centuries. And a forest shaped by the land, the river, and the wind. With unseen elk that groom the huge golf-course-green meadow at the end.

From Forks on US Highway 101, drive south about 14 miles and then turn east on the Hoh Valley Road, driving 19 miles to the Hoh Visitor Center in Olympic National Park.

Find the trail about midway off the paved loop that starts in front of the visitor center. Bear left at a T-junction in less than ¼ mile. The path here climbs to the top of a bench and then makes its way up the river, ending eventually at Mount Olympus.

In this book, the walk ends at a large green meadow fringed by forest where Mount Tom Creek enters the Hoh. A place to rest and lunch here for sure. And as you stretch out on this well-mowed grass, wonder: How do the elk do such a perfect trimming job? Every blade of grass, no matter where you rest, has been clipped the same length. No blade too long, and no blade too short. Does nature have some way of adjusting these hungry natural mowers?

You'll probably see no elk in the meadow or along the trail unless you spook one as you hike. You may see some if you camp at night, but only then if you wait quietly for them to move out of the forest to feed.

As you approach the meadow, check the mountains too. At Mount Tom Creek, note Hoh Peak slightly to the right and, at the head of the valley and the beginning of the creek, the glaciers of Mount Tom itself.

Along the way, take time to explore inviting informal paths toward the river that lead to camp and picnic spots. You can't get lost.

Moss-covered maple trees along Hoh River trail

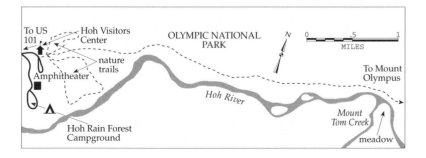

Ruby Beach

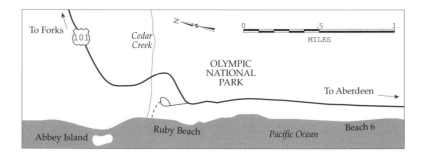

26 Ruby Beach

Features: sea stacks, beaches
One way: a few 100 yards and more
Elevation gain: 50 feet
Difficulty: easy
Open: year-round
Maps: Green Trails 163S; Custom Correct, South Olympic Coast

Too easy for any book, you say? Much too short? Yes, and yes again. But there is more here than a single beach, a single sea stack, or even a shallow eroded cave.

From Kalaloch Campground in Olympic National Park, 35 miles south of Forks on US Highway 101, drive north about 8.5 miles to a marked parking area on the ocean side of the highway.

Follow a trail off the north end of the parking area down to the beach and the outlet of Cedar Creek. Best to start here at low tides.

Walk south along the beach at low tide through an array of rocks and pools submerged at high tide. Find the modest cave here eroded in shore cliffs in less than ½ mile.

Walk north across the creek below Abbey Island, centerpiece of the offshore display here. North of the island, a beach stretches to the Hoh River and the Hoh Indian Reservation in 1¾ miles.

And do not forget nature here in the tide pools, in the water offshore, or in the skies overhead: tidal creatures in the pools, seals and whales occasionally offshore, and bald eagles often overhead.

All will signal their presence here: tide-pool creatures will move suddenly as you approach their pool, eagles may scream in the forest behind you, seals may bark and even applaud as they cruise along the beach, and whales may spout mists beyond the shore as they exhale.

And don't forget your camera. This beach has probably yielded more pictures for visitors than any other section of this coastal park strip.

27 Kalaloch Walks

Features: beaches, forest
One way: ½ mile or more
Elevation gain: slight
Difficulty: easy
Open: year-round
Maps: Green Trails 163S; Custom Correct, South Olympic Coast

Set aside an entire day to stretch these several small but different trails into a single exploration.

Find these well-used paths both north and south of Kalaloch Campground, 35 miles south of Forks, all off US Highway 101 in Olympic National Park.

Find trails to Beaches 1 and 2 along Highway 101 south of the campground. The paths here start from small parking areas on the highway, cross through forests of Sitka spruce, and end at sand beaches, which does not really tell the story. For sand beaches here vary widely from year to year. One year, after a winter storm, a beach can be strewn with uprooted trees. The next year, without the winter gales, the same beaches can stretch as barren as a well-swept floor. Yet each year each beach is worthy of new exploration. For the question is always: What's there now?

Find trails to Beaches 3 through 6 between the campground and Ruby Beach (hike 26) north of Kalaloch Campground. Here again, the condition and even the number of trails may vary year to year depending on damage caused by winter storms.

Trails to Beaches 3 and 6 lead to sand and gravel beaches often strewn with debris. (There was no trail or Beach 5 in 1994.)

The trail to Beach 4 drops over an uplifted strata of rock filled with holes bored by piddock clams (some still residing

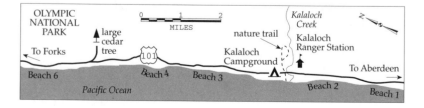

Fishing from rocks at Kalaloch Beach

there) to a beach of black sand (fishermen sometimes net smelt there) and a rock island filled with tide pools (leave all of the tide-pool life undisturbed for others yet to come).

For a sample of the rain forest here, walk a 2-mile loop trail east of Highway 101 that starts just north of the highway bridge over Kalaloch Creek, which flows between Kalaloch Campground and the Kalaloch resort. Take care when crossing the highway.

The path skirts the creek for about ½ mile before forking into a loop. No great trees here. But a fine example of a storm-embattled forest and a pleasant respite from the beach and ocean winds.

Queets River Loop trail

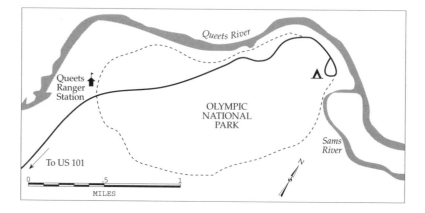

28 Queets River Loop

Features: meadows, forest, animals
One way: 2½-mile loop
Elevation gain: none
Difficulty: easy
Open: year-round
Map: Custom Correct, Queets Valley

Cross open grass meadows of long-abandoned homesteads and then several kinds of forest along the Queets River before returning to where you started. And except for elk and maybe a river otter—all by yourself.

Turn east off US Highway 101 about 7 miles south of Queets, driving 14 miles to the end of the road at Queets Campground in Olympic National Park. (As you drive, views of Mount Olympus in 2 miles and a picturesque grove of Sitka spruce and old maples beyond King's Bottom in about 6 miles.)

Start the trail from the small ranger station on the left before you reach the campground. The path starts east in front of the small station and shortly crosses open meadows. Watch for markers ahead of you. And as you walk, note the beaten patches in the grass where deer or elk have slept or rested.

As it nears the river, the trail enters a spruce forest along the river—note the rows and rows of trees growing from nurse logs—and then a jungle of moss-laden maples before reaching the campground at the end of the road. River otters are not uncommon along the river here.

Hike through the campground and pick up the trail about 25 yards back from a ford sign that marks a hiker crossing of the Queets River to a trail that continues up the other side of the river. Follow the loop-path beyond the ford sign along Sams River a short way before entering a series of smaller meadows—watch for tags and "T" markers. Walk quietly here and watch—and listen—for elk.

The loop ends on the road about 20 yards west of the ranger station.

 Big Tree Grove

Features: big trees, lush forest
One way: loops of several lengths
Elevation gain: slight
Difficulty: moderate
Open: year-round
Maps: Green Trails 197; Custom Correct, Quinault

Sadly, you're not likely to run into any big crowds here. Even though the rain-forest sample is one of the best along the coast.

Here, there are no trees named this, or trees named that. Yet the paths offer everything a good rain forest ought to offer in the abundant and disorganized manner nature has in presenting such wonders. If you are willing, of course, to take the time to look and understand.

To reach the area from US Highway 101, turn east about 37 miles north of Hoquiam onto South Shore Road along the south shore of Lake Quinault. Trails in Olympic National Forest from Willaby and Falls Creek campgrounds in 1.75 to about 2.25 miles.

Stop at the Forest Service ranger station for a detailed map of the several loops.

A ½-mile rain-forest trail, off a well-marked parking lot near

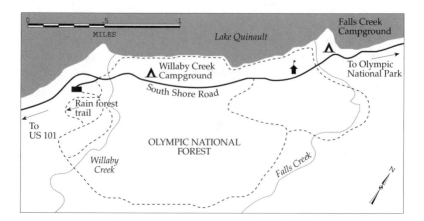

Big Tree Nature Trail

Willaby Campground, leads past identified plants and trees found throughout the forest. Offered also are views of an osprey nest.

A 2-mile loop leads through lush forest from the ranger station across Cascade and Falls creeks back to the ranger station again.

A 4-mile loop, starting from Willaby Campground or near Falls Creek Campground, offers a more thorough study of the area, including the shoreline of Lake Quinault, a cedar swamp, scenes used in displays in the Museum of Natural History in New York City, and trees, hundreds of them almost 400 years old.

A partway walk on any of these trails is worth the effort.

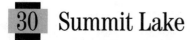 Summit Lake

Features: lake, forest, vistas, meadow
One way: 2½ miles
Elevation gain: 1,100 feet
Difficulty: moderate to steep
Open: summer
Map: Green Trails 237

Hike to a lake circled with flower meadows and tucked into a craterlike pocket atop a mountain at 5,400 feet. With views too of Mount Rainier.

From Buckley between Sumner and Enumclaw, take Highway 410 to the southwestern corner of town, turning left on Highway 162/165, and left again in about 1.75 miles onto Highway 165 to Wilkeson.

From Wilkeson, continue about 13 miles on the Carbon River

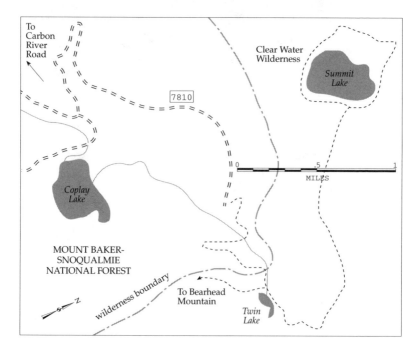

Summit Lake and Mount Rainier

Road toward the Carbon River entrance to Mount Rainier National Park. Turn left on Road 7810 just before the road reaches the park. Trailhead at the end of this poorly maintained and very rough road in more than 6 miles.

(Note: This forest road, built for logging with public funds, may be abandoned for recreational purposes by the Forest Service now that logging has ceased. Abandonment of the road would increase the hiking distance to this very popular lake by the length of the road. Write to Mount Baker–Snoqualmie National Forest.)

Find the trail at the end of the road to the left, uphill, from a parking area. The path starts through an old clear-cut (that's why there's a road) entering an old forest at the border of the Clearwater Wilderness in about ¾ mile. At Twin Lake (4,880 feet) take a trail to the left. (A trail right leads to an old lookout site on Bearhead Mountain in about 2 miles.)

The Summit Lake trail switchbacks steeply from Twin Lake to a long traverse that ends at the lake.

At Summit Lake, hike to the right for a series of camp spots in small flower meadows. Glimpses in less than ½ mile from the edge of the crater ridge down on Lily and Copley Lakes to the north (no trails) and views to the south down on Summit Lake and out at Mount Rainier.

A hike south through more meadows leads to other views of Rainier and still more places to camp. Bear grass mixed with glacier lilies and snow in late July. Fish too in the lake.

31 Ranger Falls and Green Lake

Features: forest, falls, lake
One way: 1–2 miles
Elevation gain: 1,100 feet
Difficulty: steep
Open: summer
Map: Green Trails 269

A steep 2 miles on a trail through open forest leads to a wooded mountain lake. A hike of only 1 mile, however, leads to pretty Ranger Falls on Ranger Creek.

From Buckley between Sumner and Enumclaw, take Highway 410 to the southwestern corner of town, turning left on Highway 162/165, and left again in about 1.75 miles onto Highway 165 to Wilkeson.

From Wilkeson, continue about 13 miles on the Carbon River Road to the Carbon River entrance to Mount Rainier National Park.

Find the trailhead on the right about 2 miles beyond the park entrance station.

The trail starts out steeply over rocks and roots, with short dips now and then, through an old forest of Douglas fir, hemlock,

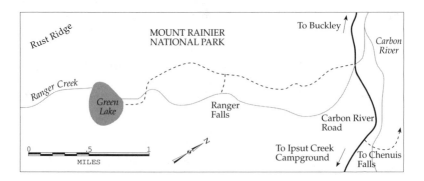

Ranger Falls

and cedar all surrounded with ferns, devil's club, and early summer offerings of salmonberries.

In about 1 mile, watch (and listen) for the waterfall downhill to the left off a switchback. A spur path drops to the falls about 100 feet below the trail.

The trail then climbs on to Green Lake, tucked in forest.

Chenuis Falls trail

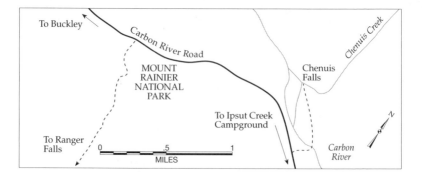

# Chenuis Falls

Features: waterfall, river
One way: ¼ mile
Elevation gain: slight
Difficulty: easy
Open: summer
Map: Green Trails 269

If you're not an old hand with mountain trails, a little effort yields lots of interest here.

From Buckley between Sumner and Enumclaw take Highway 410 to the southwestern corner of town, turning left on Highway 162/165, and left again in about 1.75 miles onto Highway 165 to Wilkeson.

From Wilkeson, continue about 13 miles on the Carbon River Road to the Carbon River entrance to Mount Rainier National Park.

Find a trailhead parking area on the left about 3.5 miles beyond the park entrance station.

The trail drops from the road and crosses the Carbon River on a log bridge or bridges that change position year to year as the gray, silted torrent weaves its way back and forth across its floodplain.

Once across the river, the trail enters a dense rain-forestlike forest to the base of the falls between grand old cedar trees that have survived who knows how many floods.

The torrent of Chenuis Creek here slides down a series of rock slabs in one grand rush to a gravel bar and wide pool, cold and clear.

Return the way you came. If you find yourself on a trail that climbs, turn back. The forest is interesting, the trail uphill is pleasant, but it goes no place at all.

 Spray Falls

Features: waterfall, vista, forest
One way: 2¼ miles or more
Elevation gain: 300 feet and more in ups and downs
Difficulty: moderate to steep
Open: summer
Map: Green Trails 269

Spray Falls is well within the limits of this book and, with its forests and viewpoints, worth the trip.

But you need to know: A struggle of another ¾ mile and up steeply another 500 feet leads to an alpine heaven in the flower meadows of Spray Park.

From Buckley between Sumner and Enumclaw, take Highway 410 to the southwestern corner of town, turning left on Highway 162/165, and left again in about 1.75 miles onto Highway 165 to Wilkeson.

Continue on Highway 165 to Mowich Lake at the end of the road in about 17 miles.

Find the trail to the falls and Spray Park downhill to the right from a hikers' walk-in camp at the end of the road. This section of the Wonderland Trail drops about ¼ mile to a junction. Turn left.

The path here wanders up and down across creeks and past mossy rock-garden slabs through ancient forest (great trees but

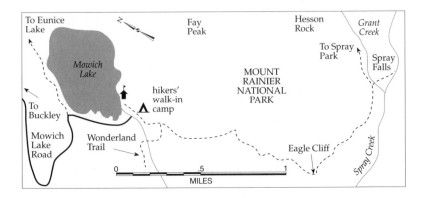

no giants, at almost 5,000 feet) to Eagle Cliff Viewpoint (signed). Follow a short path to the right to views of Mount Rainier from a rock slab high above the North Mowich River. (With luck a golden eagle may soar by.)

At about 2 miles, follow a downhill spur to the right that crosses a little stream dressed in dripping moss and yellow monkey flowers and then drops steeply to a midpoint in the falls. Note water ouzels here.

Back at the turnoff to the waterfall, the main trail now starts a steep series of switchbacks to Spray Park with its summer fields of avalanche lilies spread in the lap of Mount Rainier. (Check with rangers before you start to make sure the flowers are out and that the trail is free of snow.)

Allow time here to simply stare in awe. And wonder what all this beauty means. Seek an answer as you lunch in utter disbelief.

Eagle Cliff Viewpoint and Mount Rainier

Eunice Lake and Mount Rainier

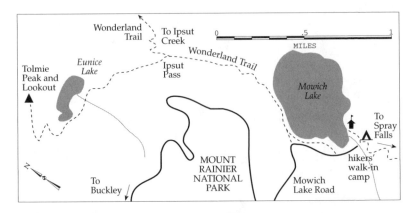

 **Eunice Lake**

Features: lake
One way: a little over 2 miles
Elevation gain: 400 feet
Difficulty: moderate
Open: summer
Map: Green Trails 269

Take your own picture of Mount Rainier reflected in the chill blue of an alpine lake surrounded by huge rock slabs and flower meadows.

From Buckley between Sumner and Enumclaw, take Highway 410 to the southwestern corner of town, turning left on Highway 162/165, and left again in about 1.75 miles onto Highway 165 to Wilkeson.

Continue on Highway 165 to Mowich Lake at the end of the road in about 17 miles.

At Mowich Lake, drop below the parking lot to a tourist path that leads left to the Wonderland Trail. Turn right on the Wonderland as it climbs gradually above the lake to a junction with the trail that leads to Eunice Lake and the Tolmie Peak Lookout. The Wonderland Trail continues on to Ipsut Creek.

From the junction, the trail drops below a series of awesome cliffs and across several rock gardens filled with penstemon and paintbrush. After crossing creeks at about the same elevation at which you started from Mowich Lake, the trail makes a sudden lunge upward over rocks and roots to the lake at 5,354 feet.

Tread carefully across rock slabs and way paths to the lakeshore through meadows filled with heather, bear grass as big as footballs, and flowers tripping all over themselves.

And don't rush away. Follow the main trail to the left and explore still more bursting small meadows and rock-slab resting places. For picture views of Mount Rainier above the lake, continue on toward Tolmie Peak Lookout, stopping at the first switchback.

The path ends at the lookout at 5,900 feet in another mile and up another 500 feet.

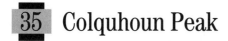 Colquhoun Peak

Features: vistas and questions
One way: ½ mile
Elevation gain: about 600 feet
Difficulty: steep
Open: summer
Map: Green Trails 239

In the distance, views of Rainier, Baker, Glacier, Stuart, and the tip of Adams. And commanding the foreground: clear-cuts, clear-cuts, clear-cuts. From the site of a former lookout at 5,173 feet.

Turn left off Highway 410 onto Greenwater Road 70 about 4 miles south of Federation State Park (20 miles from Enumclaw).

In 7 miles turn north (left) on Road 7030, following it uphill to the four-way Twin Camps junction. Bear right there on Road 7036, turning right uphill on narrow spur Road 110 in 0.3 mile. Drive to trailhead at the end in 0.6 mile.

A mossy, narrow, and sometimes brushy trail—not often used but easy to follow—leads uphill steeply. Views of clear-cuts from turning points on several switchbacks that lead to a long traverse to the former lookout site.

Enjoy the distant views here of Rainier, Baker, Glacier, and the tip of Adams and all of the flowers along the upper ridge. But then, wonder about the roads and clear-cuts you cannot avoid seeing, no matter how much you try.

And, finally, ask: What has been gained here or lost? Do the roads and clear-cuts, as some say, disrupt habitats for animals? Birds? Is there evidence of erosion along the roads? Will those replanted squares ever—even in 100 years—become part of the uncut forests around them? Will this part of the forest now, or ever, provide any benefit to the public beyond logging? Or has logging become the sole use here? Should there be a better way of managing these lands? Could some semblance of beauty have been retained? The answer is yours. For you are the owner of all you see.

Kelly Butte from Colquhoun Peak

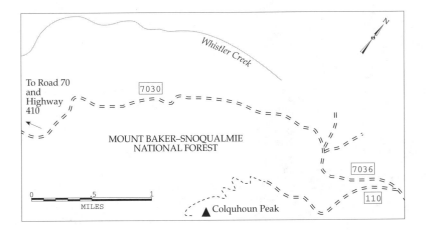

36 Greenwater Lakes

Features: rich forest, small lakes
One way: 2 miles
Elevation gain: 426 feet
Difficulty: moderate
Open: summer
Map: Green Trails 239

A quiet trail through a rich, river-bottom forest leads to two modest mountain lakes.

Drive southeast from Enumclaw on Highway 410 past Federation State Park, turning left to Road 70 about 2 miles south of Greenwater.

Find a parking area on the right in 8.8 miles from Highway 410.

Greenwater River trail

The trail starts in an old clear-cut and then drops into an older forest of Douglas fir and hemlock near the Greenwater River. In less than a mile, note the knobbly cliffs on the other side before crossing the river and then a creek (on log bridges, of course) into a grove of great old cedars. Small waterfalls off cliffs to the right.

The path climbs above a series of rapids before crossing a horse bridge over the river and on, shortly, to the first small lake with sandbars and soggy meadows. Camp spots in a cedar grove on the far side of the lake.

The trail continues climbing gradually for another ½ mile to the slightly larger lake (6 acres instead of 2) with more camp spots. The path enters the Norse Peak Wilderness about ¼ mile beyond the second lake.

Sunburst in Greenwater valley

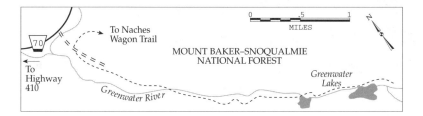

37   Goat Falls

Features: lovely falls, lovely forest
One way: ½ mile
Elevation gain: 100 feet
Difficulty: moderate to steep
Open: spring to fall
Map: White River Ranger District map (trail only)

Goat Falls

Very unlikely, this: a secret tumble of water at the end of an almost secret trail.

Drive 31.6 miles southeast of Enumclaw on Highway 410, turning east on Corral Pass Road 7174 in a little more than 0.5 mile south of the Alta Crystal Chalets or 0.4 mile north of the entrance to Silver Springs Campground.

At a T intersection in about 0.5 mile, turn right to another T intersection, turning left there and then left again in 0.2 mile onto a short spur signed Goat Falls and a parking area above a bridge over Goat Creek near holiday homes. Follow the path to the right beyond the bridge.

And the falls? You'll be bound to wonder at first. Is one of the rapids tumbling in every shape and form here

Hummingbird nest

the waterfall you seek? No. Admire each noisy rapid, yes, at the end of the short path to the creek, but press on past more big hemlocks, cedars, and snags lined with woodpecker holes.

The real falls, tumbling from one pool to another, lies in a small, dim, misty gorge at the very end of the trail. The tumbles here are bigger than the rapids you passed, yes. And yes, they are the prettiest of the lot. But, oh, they are so very, very shy.

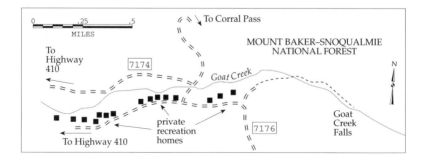

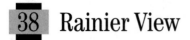 Rainier View

Features: meadows, vistas
One way: 1¼ miles
Elevation gain: 600 feet
Difficulty: moderate
Open: summer
Maps: Green Trails 239, 271

Grand, grander, grandest! Mount Rainier in all its splendor with alpine forests, flower meadows, and huckleberries too. Very popular.

Drive 31.6 miles southeast of Enumclaw on Highway 410, turning east on Corral Pass Road 7174 in a little more than 0.5 mile south of the Alta Crystal Chalets or 0.4 mile north of the entrance to Silver Springs Campground. Drive to the pass in 7 miles. Steep, narrow road. No trailers.

At the pass, bear right to a parking area and trailhead.

The trail starts in shady forest uphill across from the parking area and climbs sometimes steeply, as it must, past little meadows and even ponds. With growing glimpses of Rainier now and then along the way. Lots of elk sign as you hike but seldom any elk. Watch too for mountain goats.

After a long traverse along the east side of Castle Mountain, the trail reaches a saddle on the edge of the Norse Peak Wilder-

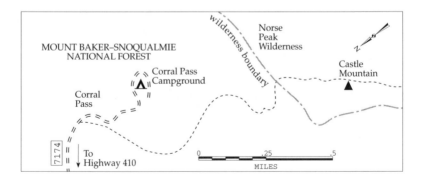

Rainier View trail toward Castle Mountain

ness. And wham! Miracle of miracles! In all her (or his?) glory:
Mount Rainier! What else is there to say?

Beyond the saddle, the path climbs to rock ledges enough for
everyone with different pictures from every ledge.

Prowl meadows here along the ridges toward Castle Mountain
for views down on the huckleberry meadows below Corral Pass.

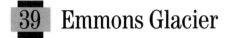 Emmons Glacier

Features: glacier, moraine, Little Tahoma Peak
One way: 2 miles
Elevation gain: 900 feet
Difficulty: easy to steep
Open: summer
Map: Green Trails 270

Look down on the dirty snout of Emmons Glacier from a windswept, desertlike moraine. With Little Tahoma Peak, third highest in the state, overwhelmed by the grandeur of Mount Rainier—except on cloudy days when it stands, for the moment, as the biggest peak around.

From Enumclaw drive about 38 miles south on Highway 410 to the White River entrance to Mount Rainier National Park, following park roads to the White River Campground 7 miles from the entrance station.

Take the Glacier Basin Trail out of the upper end of the campground. The path climbs gradually up an old abandoned mining road that still looks like one despite efforts to convert it to a trail.

In a mile turn left across a creek to the glacier trail, noticing how clear this snowmelt water is compared to the glacier-fed White River in the campground.

The path climbs along the top of a moraine created by the advancing glacier as it plowed its way down the mountain before receding to where it is today.

Note how the old bed of the glacier has come alive with new

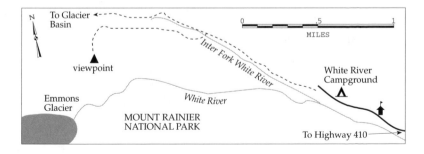

Little Tahoma and Emmons Glacier from viewpoint trail

shrubs and ponds. In 1963 a huge rock slab toppled off Little Tahoma and plummeted down the glacier at speeds of up to 300 miles an hour, carrying huge boulders, buoyed on sheets of wind compressed beneath the falling debris, to within 2,000 feet of the White River Campground. Most of the monster boulders have been buried in debris dropped since.

The end of the formal trail atop the moraine affords a view of the snout of the Emmons Glacier, its blue ice glistening beneath a blanket of gravel and rocks.

Winds here often create cyclones of sand that drift the moraine like snow. Protect cameras and binoculars from the blasts.

On days when Rainier cannot be seen, Little Tahoma Peak often proudly takes its place, for a moment at least, as the highest peak around.

 Clover Lake

Features: lakes, forest (no views of Mount Rainier)
One way: about 1½ miles
Elevation gain: 400 feet
Difficulty: easy, steep
Open: summer
Map: Green Trails 270

Not that anyone should want to leave the grand views of Mount Rainier, but a short, steep hike here leads to two pretty lakes in a lush mountain valley—with no view of Rainier at all.

From Enumclaw drive about 38 miles southeast on Highway 410 to the White River entrance to Mount Rainier National Park, following the park road to a spectacular viewpoint at Sunrise Point, 14 miles beyond the White River entrance.

From the parking area, enjoy the view out at Mount Rainier and down on the two lakes and then take the trail north of the road along the top of Sunrise Ridge. In about ¼ mile turn left to a steep trail that drops into the valley, first to Sunrise Lake and then Clover Lake. (An unmarked path continues atop the ridge to occasional clearings with new views of Rainier and out over

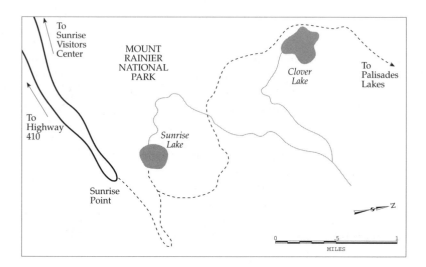

the White River valley, Goat Rocks, and Cascades. In addition to elk and deer, watch for golden eagles soaring over the valleys.)

Although Rainier may no longer be in view at the lakes, enjoy the soggy flower meadows and patches of forest between them. Elk and deer are common here. Watch for tracks.

The trail continues beyond Clover Lake to Dicks Lake Camp in another long ½ mile and to Palisades Lakes, at the end of the trail, in a total of about 3⅓ miles.

Sunrise Lake

Mount Rainier from Silver Forest trail

 Silver Forest

Features: blanched trees, grand vistas
One way: 1 mile or more
Elevation gain: slight
Difficulty: easy
Open: summer
Map: Green Trails 270

There are constant views of Mount Rainier, yes. But the views here: framed by gnarled, sometimes fallen silver ghosts of alpine trees killed by fire and then bleached by the sun.

From Enumclaw drive about 38 miles southeast on Highway 410 to the White River entrance to Mount Rainier National Park, following the spectacular park road 14 miles to its end at Sunrise.

From the southern, mountain-side of the big parking lot, take the trail downhill for about 100 yards to the Emmons Vista overviews.

Turn left past the overviews (stop to look, most certainly) and continue to the silver forest in about ½ mile. Continuing vistas here of the mountain through the bleached, silver ghosts of pine and subalpine fir as the trail wends its way through the huge, once-burned meadow.

No crowds here. Often on this huge meadow you may find yourself alone with the mountain, the meadow flowers—lots and lots of them—and with elk and deer and hawks and eagles too.

This path continues more than a mile across what's known as Yakima Park below the park road and Yakima Ridge. Go as far as you want and stop as often as you like just to soak up this magnificent scene. (Most visitors here, poor souls, stop at the formal vista overviews.)

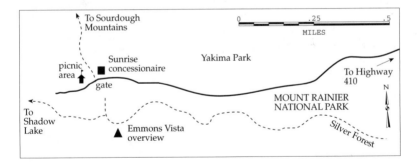

Shadow Lake

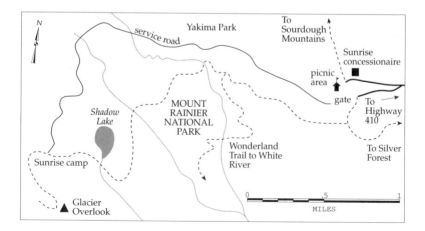

 Shadow Lake

Features: vistas, forest, lake
One way: about 1½ miles
Elevation gain: 190 feet
Difficulty: moderate
Open: summer
Maps: Green Trails 270; Sunrise Quadrangle (7.5-minute series)

Walk through subalpine forest and across flower meadows to a pretty mountain lake—all in the awesome presence of Mount Rainier.

From Enumclaw drive about 38 miles southeast on Highway 410 to the White River entrance to Mount Rainier National Park, following the spectacular park road 14 miles to its end at Sunrise.

Find the broad trail downhill below the entrance of the large parking lot, turning right in about 100 yards to the Sunrise Rim Trail, which drops gradually to a junction with the Wonderland Trail in ½ mile.

Continue ahead (the Wonderland Trail to the left drops to White River Campground), turning left in less than ¼ mile to Shadow Lake and Sunrise Camp, a walk-in camp.

The trail passes small tarns, crosses a creek (note the wet-rooted flowers), and circles a knoll to the outlet of the 4-acre lake at 5,800 feet. Views of Little Tahoma Peak, third highest in the state, from the shore. Rainier hides behind a ridge.

If you have the time, hike on up the trail another ¼ mile and 200 feet in elevation to a grand view from Glacier Overlook.

Return the way you came. Other paths lead up old gated roads to the ranger station and parking area.

43 Dege Peak

Features: flower meadows, sweeping vistas
One way: 2 miles
Elevation gain: 600 feet
Difficulty: moderate to steep
Open: summer
Maps: Green Trails 270; Sunrise Quadrangle (7.5-minute series)

Outrageous views of Mount Rainier, most certainly. But from the top of Dege Peak (7,006 feet), views too of the Cascades from north to south, the Olympics, and, at your feet, Clover and Sunrise lakes and the tarns of Huckleberry Creek.

From Enumclaw drive about 38 miles southeast on Highway 410 to the White River entrance to Mount Rainier National Park, following the spectacular park road either to the parking and viewing area at Sunrise Point or to the end of the road at Sunrise, 14 miles beyond the White River entrance. Trails lead to the peak from both locations. The trail from Sunrise is preferred.

From Sunrise find the trail off the parking lot north (uphill) beside the rest room (the heavily used path across this huge meadow is steeper than it looks).

In mid-meadow fork to the right, bearing to the right again to the Sourdough Ridge Trail on the side of Sourdough Mountains. As the path here makes its way through clumps of stunted trees and open meadow, note the animal trails that drop from the ridge. Elk here seek respite from summer flies in the wind that sweeps the exposed ridge above you, dropping across the trail on cool evenings to feed in the meadows.

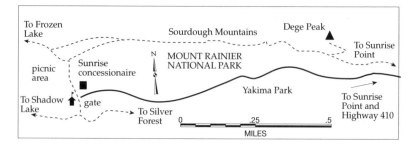

Mount Rainier from Dege Peak

As it nears Dege Peak, the trail crosses narrow saddles, affording views to the north into valleys filled with tarns, ponds, and meadows.

The ⅓-mile spur up Dege Peak forks to the left and then plugs along up its well-designed switchbacks to a flat viewing area at the top. Again: views from Mount Baker to Mount Adams with the smog of Seattle in between. And with Rainier, naturally.

To reach the top of the peak from the parking and viewing area at Sunrise Point, find the 1½-mile trail up the Sourdough Ridge Trail across the road off the uphill end of the parking area. This path climbs sharply with views down on Clover and Sunrise lakes (hike 40) and out at Rainier.

 44 Mount Fremont Lookout

Features: vistas
One way: 2⅘ miles
Elevation gain: 800 feet
Difficulty: easy to steep
Open: midsummer
Maps: Green Trails 270; Sunrise Quadrangle (7.5-minute series)

A lookout here manned by a ranger who can identify all of the scenery you see and explain all of the equipment it takes to maintain such a high and spectacular fire watch.

(Check at the Sunrise Ranger Station before you start, to determine if the lookout is manned. If that's important to you.)

View from Mount Fremont Lookout

From Enumclaw drive about 38 miles southeast on Highway 410 to the White River entrance to Mount Rainier National Park, following the spectacular park road to the end at Sunrise in 14 miles beyond the White River entrance.

Find the trailhead behind the rest room at the far end of the large parking lot.

The path starts up across a deceptively steep meadow before forking left to the Sourdough Ridge Trail and a viewpoint and resting places atop the ridge (at a junction with the Forest Lake trail), with sweeping vistas to the north.

The trail now makes a long traverse along the south side of the ridge before reaching fenced Frozen Lake, a park water source, and a junction with the Wonderland Trail.

At a junction with the lookout and Burroughs Mountain trails just beyond the lake (whistle at the marmots here), turn right on a trail that climbs over barren alpine slopes to the lookout at 7,181 feet.

As you walk, don't ignore the flowers that bloom on these barren slopes against all odds. The marmots and pikas here will call attention to themselves.

From the lookout tower see Rainier, naturally, look down on the vast expanses of Grand Park, and to the north glimpse a corner of Puget Sound, the Olympics, and Seattle's crown of smog.

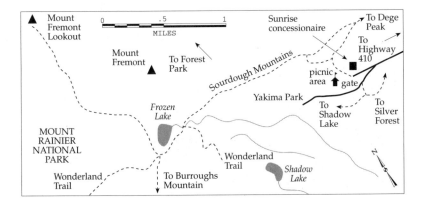

45 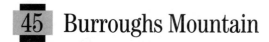 Burroughs Mountain

Features: vistas, alpine plateau
One way: 2 miles, more or less
Elevation gain: 900 feet, more or less
Difficulty: moderate to steep
Open: late summer
Maps: Green Trails 270; Sunrise Quadrangle (7.5-minute series)

Hike through the gates of heaven here into the vast beauty not only of Mount Rainier but also of the barren expanse of an austere alpine plateau.

From Enumclaw drive about 38 miles southeast on Highway 410 to the White River entrance to Mount Rainier National Park, following the spectacular park road to the end at Sunrise in 14 miles beyond the White River entrance.

Find the trailhead behind the rest room at the far end of the large parking lot.

The path starts up across a deceptively steep meadow before forking left to the Sourdough Ridge Trail and a viewpoint and resting places atop the ridge (at a junction with the Forest Lake trail), with sweeping vistas to the north.

The path now makes a long traverse along the south side of the ridge before reaching fenced Frozen Lake, a park water source, and, just beyond, the junction with the Burroughs Mountain and Mount Fremont Lookout trails.

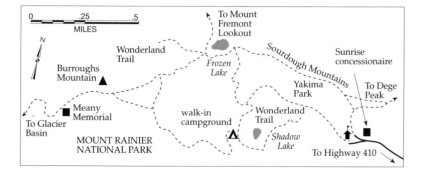

Ground squirrel on the barren slopes of Burroughs Mountain

The trail up Burroughs Mountain climbs to the left across a barren slope to a junction with a trail that leads down to Shadow Lake.

From here on the choice is yours. Follow the trail another ½ mile to more grand views from a memorial at 7,400 feet to Edmund S. Meany, University of Washington historian and one-time president of The Mountaineers. Or tenderly pick your way across the rocky plateau to marvel at the alpine flowers that struggle there. Or look out on great meadow "parks" to the north, the higher ridges to the west, the glories of Rainier to the south, and down on Sunrise to the east.

Pack a lunch for sure. Carry water. And allow every moment you can find to soak up the essence of this vast plateau.

Return the way you came or take longer routes down to Shadow Lake and back up to the parking lot or down to the White River and the campground there.

Chinook Creek falls

46 Deer Creek Falls

Features: waterfalls and forest
One way: ¼ mile
Elevation gain: less than 100 feet
Difficulty: steep
Open: summer
Map: Green Trails 270

A waterfall surprise guarded by huge and ancient cedars, hemlocks, and Douglas fir just below Highway 123.

Drive 40 miles southeast of Enumclaw to Cayuse Pass on Highway 410. At the pass, continue south on Highway 123. After passing through the tunnel, find a small unmarked parking area on the left 1 mile beyond the big Deer Creek bridge, near Milepost 12 just as the highway rounds a point. Note a small "EASTSIDE TRAIL" sign on the right side of the road.

From the highway (use care in crossing the road) the trail drops immediately into rich old forest to the first overview near a huge Douglas fir. The second point in a few yards more, guarded by cedars and hemlock, offers fuller views from the railed trail.

The waterfall, a torrent in the spring and a wisp of water in the fall, tumbles from one pool to another and then slides over a rock to the bottom of a gorge.

Not for undisciplined children. No trail to the bottom of the falls.

The path continues ½ mile down to a bridge across Chinook Creek (soon to join the Ohanapecosh River) with noisy rapids and lots of places to lunch. Paths here lead both up and down the creek and up to Owyhigh Lakes in another 5 miles.

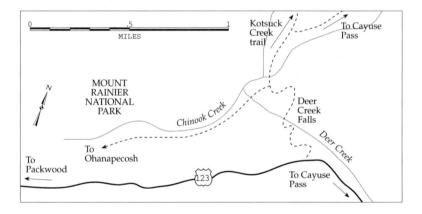

 Naches Peak Loop

Features: flower meadows, tarns, vistas
One way: 3-mile loop
Elevation gain: 400 feet
Difficulty: easy to moderate
Open: late summer
Maps: Green Trails 270, 271

From glacier lilies in the spring to hooded pasque flowers in the fall—all high on the Cascade crest around Naches Peak.

From Enumclaw drive southeast 43 miles on Highway 410 to Chinook Pass, finding the trailhead off a parking/rest-room area to the left just beyond the Pacific Crest Trail bridge over the highway.

Find the trail uphill to the left of the rest rooms, turning left on the Pacific Crest Trail and following it over the bridge above the highway.

The trail, at nearly 6,000 feet, clings to Naches Peak as it enters the William O. Douglas Wilderness to wend its way through meadows and past small tarns before climbing to a junction where the Crest Trail drops left to Dewey Lake and beyond.

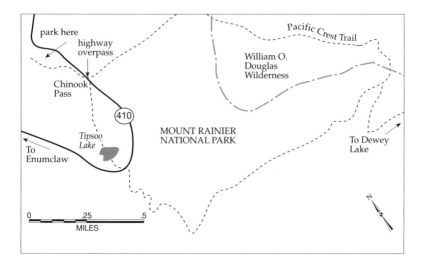

Mount Rainier from Naches Peak trail

Bear right at the junction, pausing in the meadow there long enough to look down on the lake and out at Mount Rainier, your constant host for the rest of the hike.

Again, the trail winds through meadows and past still more tarns before dropping down to Highway 410 above Tipsoo Lake. Take time en route to explore unmarked way trails to the left that lead to special vista points. Walk back on the highway to your car.

And be sure to take your flower book. Alpine bouquets here change week by week. Marmots, pikas, elk. Even goats here too. Note their occasional dusting patches where they dust themselves on slopes below the trail.

Pacific Crest Trail north of Chinook Pass

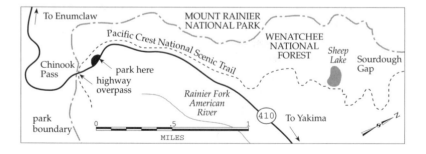

48 Sheep Lake

Features: high forest, meadows, lake
One way: 2 miles
Elevation gain: 400 feet
Difficulty: moderate
Open: midsummer
Map: Green Trails 270

Hike through huckleberry fields and mountain hemlock forests, all above 5,500 feet, to a meadow lake you'll wish you could take home.

From Enumclaw drive southeast 43 miles on Highway 410 to Chinook Pass, finding the trailhead off a parking/rest-room area to the left just beyond the Pacific Crest Trail bridge over the highway.

Find the trail uphill to the left of the rest rooms, turning right on the Pacific Crest Trail in 100 yards or so.

The Crest Trail here climbs across steep huckleberry slopes above Highway 410 for a mile with sweeping views to the south (the highway goes down as the trail climbs gently up) before turning north into open forest.

The trail continues its gradual climb past small meadows and around outcrops of rock, breaking out suddenly at the pretty lake set just below the crest of the Cascades at 5,700 feet.

Camp and picnic spots along the shore and among trees above the lake. A popular hiking destination for backpacking families.

The Crest Trail continues north to Sourdough Gap and beyond.

 49 Twin Sisters Lakes

Features: two lakes, berries, beaches
One way: 1½ miles or more
Elevation gain: 600 feet
Difficulty: moderate
Open: summer
Maps: Green Trails 271, 303

Two lakes on a high plateau in the William O. Douglas Wilderness surrounded by huckleberry fields, little beaches, and views.

From Yakima drive west on Highway 410, or from Enumclaw drive 23 miles east from the junction of highways 410 and 123 over Chinook Pass. In both instances, turn south at American River to Bumping Lake Road 18 (or 1800, depending on the sign).

At the end of the paved road continue on Road 18/1800 to a junction with Road 1808. (Road 18/1800 turns right there to Lily and Granite lakes.) Follow Road 1808 to the left to its end at the small Deep Creek Campground. (Ignore Twin Sisters trail signs at a horse camp a mile before you get there.) Twenty miles from Highway 410. Find the trail off the end of the campground.

The campground path switchbacks quickly into the William O. Douglas Wilderness, climbing erratically through an open forest of spruce and mountain hemlock above Deep Creek before topping a ridge and dropping down to the first and most personal of the twin lakes, at 5,200 feet.

Stop here to enjoy the huckleberries, small sandy beaches,

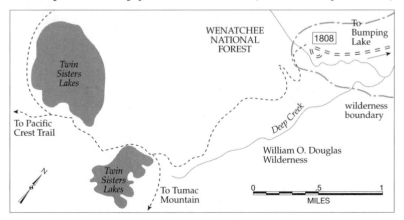

coves, meadows, and view of cone-shaped Tumac Mountain, a constant reference point from all the trails here.

To reach the largest and most lakelike of the twin lakes, follow the trail ½ mile to the right along the shore of the small lake and over a slight huckleberry rise.

Informal spurs lead to the big lake and glimpses of Mount Adams. A spur turns north along the west side of the lake as the main path continues on past several ponds to the Pacific Crest Trail and beyond.

This area, laced with trails, ponds, and meadows, was a favorite of Supreme Court Justice William O. Douglas. He roamed this area from Yakima as a boy, spent many of his summers near it as a judge, and wrote of it extensively in his book *My Wilderness, the Pacific West* (Doubleday & Company, 1960).

Read it with a map before you hike here to benefit from the secrets he enjoyed.

Twin Sisters Lakes trail

Boulder Cave

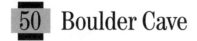 Boulder Cave

Features: lava cave, waterfall
One way: ¾ mile
Elevation gain: about 300 feet
Difficulty: moderate
Open: summer
Map: Green Trails 272

Discover a hidden waterfall before exploring a dark and musty 400-foot tunnel/cave along Devil Creek.

Drive east from Yakima on Highway 410, or south from Enumclaw on Highway 410 over Chinook Pass. Turn right in both instances across the Naches River on the Cliffdell Bridge, about 27 miles from Chinook Pass or 3.3 miles southeast of the junction with the Little Naches Road.

Beyond the bridge, turn right and then right again onto Road 1704 to the Boulder Cave picnic area, 1.2 miles from the highway.

From the picnic area, follow a heavily used trail uphill. The trail climbs above Devil Creek canyon before dropping down to the falls and the mouth of the cave.

At the bottom of the canyon, cross the creek and climb upstream to the right over rocks to a waterfall tumbling through a gash in the cliff.

The mouth of the cave, 200 feet wide and 50 feet high, hangs over the creek like a monstrous hood. The cave was cut by the creek through collapsed lava-flow basalts.

Best to bring a flashlight. Much of the cavern is dark due to twists and turns. And wear your hiking shoes. The path follows Devil Creek through the cave to an exit and then loops back to the trail.

Two warnings. Don't throw anything into the canyon—others may be exploring below you—and watch for falling rock.

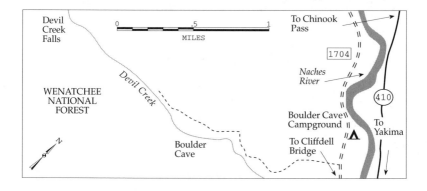

Cora Lake

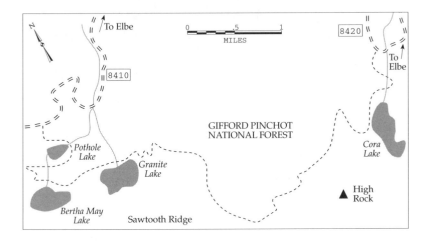

51 Bertha May and Granite Lakes

Features: mountain lakes
One way: 2 miles
Elevation gain: about 600 feet
Difficulty: moderate
Open: summer
Map: Green Trails 301

Three lakes on one trail with a view at the end of Mount Rainier. All at above 4,000 feet.

From Puyallup, drive south on Highway 161 through Eatonville to Highway 7 and the small community of Elbe. From Elbe follow Highway 706 east about 10 miles (some 3 miles west of the entrance to Mount Rainier National Park), turning south on Road 52.

Cross the Nisqually River bridge and turn left (east), continuing past the Big Creek Campground, turning right onto Road 84 in about 3.25 miles, and right again in 1.25 miles, onto Road 8410.

Find the trail to the left off a parking area and camp spot on a curve in 3.8 miles. If you pass a sign saying "NOT MAINTAINED BEYOND THIS POINT," you've gone too far.

The path drops from the left side of the parking area and bears to the right above Pothole Lake. At an unmarked old logging road junction, turn left around the lake.

After a quick spurt uphill beyond the lake outlet, the trail climbs through big hemlock and Douglas fir to a trail junction. Turn left there as the path switchbacks to a long traverse that ends at Bertha May Lake (4,055 feet). Way trails drop to the lake.

The path continues above the lake, climbing to Granite Lake (4,175 feet). Follow the path to a point above the outlet of the lake for views over the valley and Mount Rainier. If you tire of looking at the mountain, turn and watch the birds on the lake.

The path continues on to Cora Lake in another long mile.

 **High Rock Lookout**

Features: breathtaking views
One way: 1¾ miles
Elevation gain: about 1,300 feet
Difficulty: steep
Open: late summer
Map: Green Trails 301

Climb to the edge of heaven at 5,685 feet and stand face to face with Mount Rainier. And dare to say you're not awed by the wonder of it all.

From Puyallup, drive south on Highway 161 through Eatonville to Highway 7 and the small community of Elbe. From Elbe follow Highway 706 east about 10 miles (some 3 miles west of the entrance to Mount Rainier National Park), turning south on Road 52.

After crossing the Nisqually River bridge, either 1) drive straight ahead on paved Road 85 as it circles to the right and back again to Road 8440, reaching the trailhead at Towhead Gap in 11 miles, or 2) turn left on Road 85 past the Big Creek Campground, turning right onto Road 84 in about 3.25 miles, reaching the trailhead on Road 8440 at Towhead Gap in 10 miles. In either case, note your lookout destination high above you to the west before you start your climb.

The trail here makes no bones about it as it climbs straight

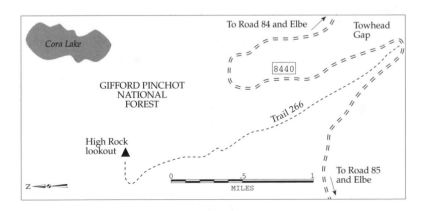

High Rock Lookout from the air

up the ridge to the old lookout, once abandoned by the Forest Service and for a number of years maintained by hikers who loved the place. It's now sometimes manned by the agency from mid-July to mid-September, depending on the weather, with observers who can help you appreciate the grandeur of all you see.

The building sits perched on the very edge of a precipice on top of Sawtooth Ridge with nothing between you and Rainier and the fistful of lakes below. With Adams, St. Helens, Hood, the Cascades, and Olympics there too on the clearest days.

Not for the jittery or uncontrolled. Only for the devoted and those eager to bow in reverence to all of the natural wonders there.

 Carter Falls

Features: forest, waterfall
One way: 1 mile
Elevation gain: about 400 feet
Difficulty: easy to moderate
Open: summer
Map: Green Trails 269

From a busy campground and roaring river, hike a broad and heavily used path to a once-tamed waterfall now running free.

From the Nisqually entrance at the southwestern corner of Mount Rainier National Park, drive past Longmire to a Wonderland Trail junction across the road from Cougar Rock Campground. (The trail to the right drops down to Longmire.)

To see the falls, follow the branch ahead as it drops below the road to a log bridge across the Nisqually River and then climbs along the Paradise River toward Paradise.

The broad path here was once a road built to service a generating plant powered by water from above the falls. As you walk through the forest, note remnants of the wire-wrapped wooden flume that carried water to a private powerhouse near the Nisqually River.

You can't miss the falls. Like all good waterfalls, it shouts its presence before you see it. Viewpoints on the trail.

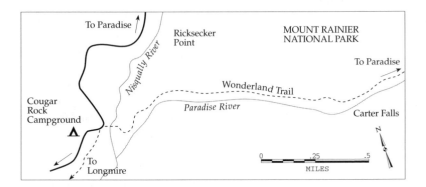

Mount Rainier and footbridge over the Nisqually River

The trail continues on to Narada Falls and, eventually, through much forest and many meadows, to Paradise, climbing in 4 miles a total of 2,200 feet from the campground. (If you must, it's wiser to start at the top and hike down.)

Comet Falls

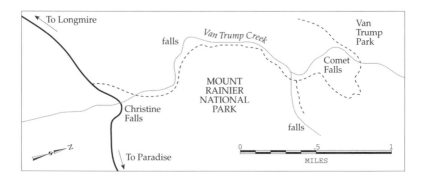

54 Comet Falls

Features: towering falls, musical creek
One way: 2 miles
Elevation gain: 1,200 feet
Difficulty: moderate to steep
Open: summer
Map: Green Trails 269

The 320-foot Comet Falls is reason enough to start up this trail. But the clattering music of the creek, the occasional winks from Mount Rainier, and the extra-shy falls near the end make the trip imperative.

From the Nisqually entrance of Mount Rainier National Park, drive 10.3 miles toward Paradise, finding a parking area for the trailhead to Van Trump Park to the left. (If you pass Christine Falls, plunging through its gorge just off the road, you've gone too far.)

The trail starts to the right of the parking area, enters forest, and crosses Van Trump Creek. Pause here to note the bowls etched in rock below the wooden bridge and the small stones in every bowl that still perform the etching.

Beyond the small bridge the trail turns musical as bells and xylophones join a cacophony of timpani, cymbals, and castanets from small waterfalls gushing over, around, under, and between rock fissures in the creek. With crescendos fading diminuendo as the trail switchbacks above and then away from the creek.

Midway, the path crosses a rock field to more switchbacks, turning finally to a bridge at a fork in the creek. At the bridge, look upstream to your right. A three-step waterfall in its own private gorge. Worth a trip all by itself if it were not for Comet Falls suddenly, in just a few yards more, pluming in great leaps and bounds from Van Trump Park.

Pick your own best view of Comet Falls from informal viewpoints on and below the trail.

Take all of your pictures here. The path climbs sharply now to Van Trump Park in another mile.

55 Nisqually Glacier

Features: flower meadows, glacier, vistas
One way: 1 mile and more
Elevation gain: 300 feet and more
Difficulty: easy to moderate
Open: midsummer
Map: Green Trails 270S

Views of Nisqually Glacier may be the goal but the spectacle of flower meadows, deer, and Mount Rainier in all her glory overwhelms it all.

From the Nisqually entrance to Mount Rainier National Park, drive 19 miles to the visitor center at Paradise, stopping all along the way for view-on-view-on-view of Mount Rainier.

Paradise visitor center

The Nisqually Vista and Moraine trails (among many) lead to views down on the glacial ice-field source of the Nisqually River.

The **Nisqually Vista Trail** loops a mile from the visitor center, dropping 200 feet gradually across meadows (deer here for sure) and past a fairy pool to a viewpoint looking out at the glacier's snout and down on the moraine left by the glacier as it receded.

Meadows here can be covered with snow until mid-July, with the most brilliant displays of flowers during the first two weeks of August.

The **Moraine Trail** leads to views (and flowers too) at 5,700 feet down on the glacier with its crevasses, icefalls, and moraines. Note the glacial blue ice beneath the piles of gravel littering the top of the glacier. Here on warm days you can hear the massive ice field crack and groan as it grinds its way down the mountain.

To reach this trail from the visitor center, follow the Nisqually Vista Trail to a junction with the Dead Horse Creek Trail, turning right and dropping down to the Moraine Trail in more than another ½ mile.

Barren country here. Yet as you walk the moraine, note how tiny flowers persist in growing there. And, of course, all this beneath the massive Mount Rainier.

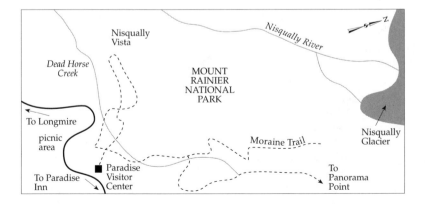

Tatoosh Range from Panorama Point

 Panorama Point

Features: flowers, vistas
One way: 2½ miles
Elevation gain: 1,400 feet
Difficulty: moderate to steep
Open: late summer
Map: Green Trails 207S

Hike to the very edge of heaven where Mount Rainier's awesome grandeur and brazen power humbles all and man's problems come to naught.

From the Nisqually entrance to Mount Rainier National Park, drive 19 miles to Paradise, finding trails either from the visitor center or farther up the road from the large Paradise parking lot near the ranger station.

From the visitor center, take the Dead Horse Creek Trail a little more than 1 mile to a junction at about 6,100 feet with the Skyline Trail which starts its uphill climb from the Paradise parking lot.

Flowers dominate the lower meadows. As the snow melts, white avalanche lilies claim the meadows with other flowers following in a rolling procession of color that lasts until fall when reds and yellows predominate.

Only the hardiest flowers survive on the higher, barren alpine slopes as the trail loops to a glacier vista before settling down to a steep, steady climb to Panorama Point.

As the name suggests: a panorama. From Rainier above you to Mount Adams, what's left of Mount St. Helens, Mount Hood, the Goat Rocks, and, at your feet, the Nisqually Glacier and the meadows of Paradise, of course.

Return the way you came unless rangers report the trails beyond the point clear of steep snow.

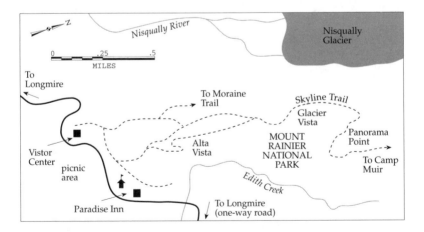

57 Stevens–Van Trump Historical Monument

Features: waterfalls, high meadows, vista
One way: about 2 miles
Elevation gain: 600 feet
Difficulty: moderate to steep
Open: late summer
Map: Green Trails 270S

Pause at a pretty waterfall and then walk on to a monument honoring the first climbers of Mount Rainier who started their climb there in 1870. With flower meadows and grand vistas all along the way.

From the Nisqually entrance to Mount Rainier National Park, drive 19 miles to Paradise, taking the main Skyline Trail uphill to the right from the large Paradise parking lot near the ranger station.

The heavily used trail, paved at the start, climbs in about ½ mile to Myrtle Falls which threads over a cascade of rocks beneath a trail bridge. Take a way trail to the right for a full view of the falls.

The trail then wends a mile across spectacular meadows to

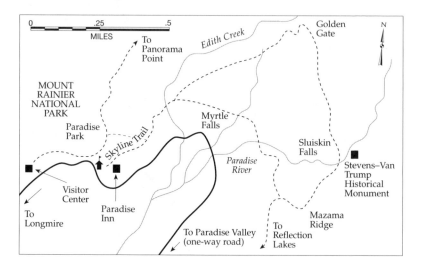

Mount Rainier and Myrtle Falls

cross the Paradise River, switchbacking there to the top of a
ridge and on to the monument (6,000 feet). It was at this monument that Hazard Stevens, son of Washington's first governor,
and P. B. Van Trump started their climb of the mountain after
being guided there by Sluiskin, an Indian guide.

Take time here to savor the splendor of the meadows and
then return either the way you came or hike on, down and then
up again, to Golden Gate (6,400 feet), turning left there down the
Golden Gate trail to Myrtle Falls.

Or, if you can arrange to have someone pick you up by car,
return down the Mazama Ridge trail to Reflection Lakes (see
hike 58, Faraway Rock).

58   Faraway Rock

Features: meadows, vistas, ponds
One way: 3-mile loop and more
Elevation gain: 400 feet plus
Difficulty: moderate to steep
Open: late summer
Map: Green Trails 270S

Hike on a loop of trails from Reflection Lakes through meadows and forest past tarns and ponds to Faraway Rock, visible high above the lakes to the northeast even as you start.

From the Nisqually entrance to Mount Rainier National Park, drive 19 miles up the Nisqually road to a junction with the Stevens Canyon Road and then on to Reflection Lakes. From the Stevens Canyon entrance to the park, drive about 16 miles to the lakes.

At the largest lake, start to the left on the Wonderland Trail as it winds below the parking strip above the shore of the lake.

At a junction where the Wonderland Trail turns left, turn right across soggy meadows onto the Lakes Trail as it climbs sharply to the top of Mazama Ridge at 5,400 feet.

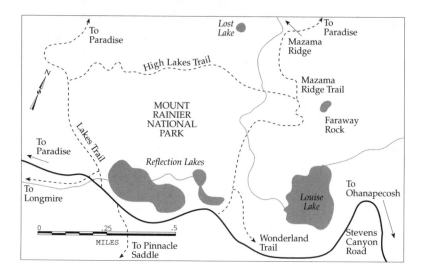

Tatoosh Range and Artist Pool located at Faraway Rock

Turn right at the crest of the ridge onto the High Lakes Trail and follow the path up through forest and more meadows to the Mazama Ridge trail in 1¼ miles.

If you have the time, wander north on the Mazama Ridge trail for ½ mile or so to more lovely meadows being watched over by Rainier. Otherwise, turn right to Faraway Rock with its adjoining pond and airplane views over Reflection Lakes and Louise Lake at your feet. Don't ignore the other tarns along the trail.

From Faraway Rock the trail drops sharply to a creek and then on to a junction with the Wonderland Trail. Bear right to Reflection Lakes. Taking time, of course, to frame a picture of Rainier reflected in the lakes.

 Pinnacle Saddle

Features: vistas and more vistas
One way: 1⅓ miles
Elevation gain: 1,000 feet
Difficulty: steep but steady
Open: late summer
Map: Green Trails 270S

You'll have to work here, yes. But the end result atop Tatoosh Ridge is worth every step, and every groan.

From the Nisqually entrance to Mount Rainier National Park, drive 19 miles up the Nisqually road to the Stevens Canyon Road and then on to Reflection Lakes. From the Stevens Canyon entrance to the park, drive about 16 miles to the lakes.

Find the trail, uphill to the south, from the parking area along the largest Reflection Lake. (Early in the summer, ask rangers about possible snow hazards on the trail before you start.)

The path here starts in forest south of the road, crosses a small stream decorated with gentians and monkey flowers, hurries up a few steps, rounds a small meadow or two, and then settles down to a well-planned trudge across a scree face of Pinnacle Peak to a saddle between Denman and Pinnacle peaks on the crest of the Tatoosh Range.

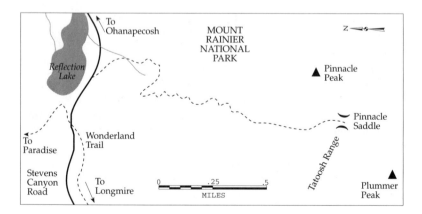

One of the most spectacular views in this book is the one here of Mount Rainier and Paradise. And to the south over a meadow to Mount Adams, the Goat Rocks, and beyond.

Trails along ridges left or right look inviting, but unless you are properly equipped and experienced, they are best ignored or explored with extreme care. Non-climbers can get in serious trouble dodging falling rocks on the slippery cliffs of Pinnacle Peak.

A short hike downhill beyond the saddle leads to a meadow and sometime tarn.

Pinnacle Saddle trail and Mount Rainier

Snow Lake and Mount Rainier

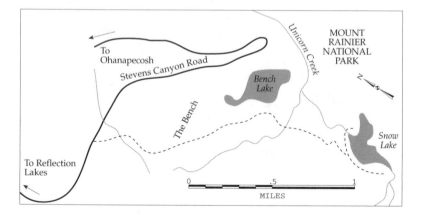

60 Snow Lake

Features: lakes, meadows, mountains
One way: 1½ miles
Elevation gain: 200 feet
Difficulty: moderate to steep
Open: late summer
Map: Green Trails 270S

Hike to views down on one lake and then on and up to a second tucked in a cirque below Unicorn Glacier and Unicorn Peak (6,917 feet). With views of Mount Rainier along the way.

From the Nisqually entrance to Mount Rainier National Park, drive 19 miles up the Nisqually road to a junction with the Stevens Canyon Road. Find the trailhead on the right beyond Reflection Lakes, about 6 miles from the junction. From the Stevens Canyon entrance to the park, drive about 13 miles to the trailhead on the left.

The path climbs away from the road in short spurts, drops over a creek, and climbs sharply again to a rolling swampy meadow filled with elephant head flowers and cotton grass in season and signs of elk and deer. The path drops down a clutch of steps (there are a number of untrail-like steps along the trail) to a viewpoint down on Bench Lake and out at Rainier. A stub trail drops and ends at the edge of the lake.

From the viewpoint, the trail drops down more steps to another creek and switchbacks (still more steps with views of Rainier behind you) to a short meadowed draw along Unicorn Creek.

At a junction, bear left along the top of a ridge above Snow Lake to a spur of rock slabs on the right. Camp there by permit only. The path to the right continues toward the head of the lake with views up at cliff walls, waterfalls, and patches of snow.

 Martha Falls

Features: waterfall, forest
One way: ¾ mile
Elevation gain: about 500 feet
Difficulty: moderate
Open: late summer
Map: Green Trails 270

A lovely waterfall most likely to be yours alone on a downhill stretch of the Wonderland Trail in Stevens Canyon.

From the Nisqually entrance to Mount Rainier National Park, drive 19 miles up the Nisqually road to the Stevens Canyon Road, driving right past Reflection Lakes and above Louise Lake to a downhill hairpin turn to the left. Find the trailhead in 0.7 mile from the sharp turn, on the right off a small parking spot on the shoulder where the Wonderland Trail crosses the road.

The path here drops steadily through forest to a bridge over Unicorn Creek which flows out of Snow Lake higher on the mountain. Glimpses through the trees of the Stevens Canyon Road below.

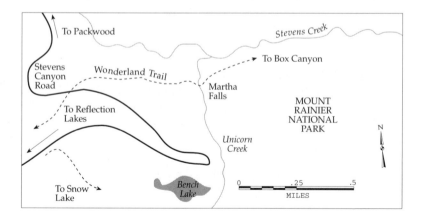

Beyond the bridge, a path leads (right) to the base of the falls. A worthy trophy for any waterfall collector. And a welcome, noisy, refreshing, and lovely respite for hikers struggling up the Wonderland Trail toward Paradise. You can see the falls from the Stevens Canyon Road, high to the right, if you drive on to the Stevens Canyon entrance. No paths to the top of the falls.

Martha Falls

62 Box Canyon

Features: glacial footprints, gorge
One way: ½-mile loop
Elevation gain: slight
Difficulty: easy
Open: summer
Map: Green Trails 270

The time of man amounts to less than an instant here amid the still-unfinished efforts of persistent nature.

As you walk, look at the work of the glacier that etched and shaped the huge rock slabs along the trail and then peer into a gorge still being eroded by a stream.

From the Nisqually entrance of Mount Rainier National Park, drive 25 miles up the Nisqually road and down the Stevens Canyon Road. Or from the Stevens Canyon entrance, drive 10 miles up the Stevens Canyon Road.

Find the loop trail along a rail fence across the road from a well-signed formal Box Canyon display.

The trail leads past slabs of rock rounded and etched centuries ago by the Cowlitz Glacier as it ground its way down the mountain and then retreated miles and miles and thousands of feet up the mountain to where it is today.

Nature has not been able to cover all of the violence. But mosses, lichens, grasses, and flowers have already established footholds in cracks, striations, and fissures left by the moving ice.

At the junction with the Wonderland Trail, turn downhill across a trail bridge over the narrow gorge of the Muddy Fork of the Cowlitz River. Here, more than 100 feet below you, the river turns on edge as it continues eroding its way into the mountain's lava below spray-drenched walls draped with ferns and struggling flowers.

Continue on the Wonderland Trail to the Stevens Canyon Road and the parking area for the loop trip, or return the way you came.

Take time to view Mount Adams to the south from a viewpoint off the parking area.

Glacier striations (scratches), before they were covered by moss or chipped away for interpretive signs

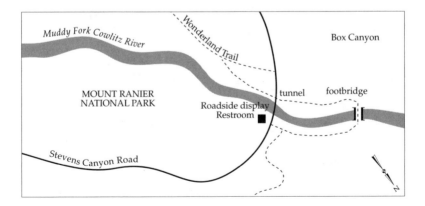

 Silver Falls

Features: waterfall
One way: 1 mile or less
Elevation gain: slight
Difficulty: easy
Open: spring to fall
Maps: Green Trails 270, 302

Rich forest, a hot soda-water spring, and as a climax: a roaring waterfall.

From Enumclaw or Yakima take Highway 410 to Cayuse Pass, driving south 12 miles on Highway 123 to the Ohanapecosh Campground in the southeastern corner of Mount Rainier National Park.

Find the trail behind the visitor center or off the end of the first spur road to the right just beyond the visitor center.

Follow either of the trails through rich forest, taking time at the start for a side trip to a hot spring where soda water bubbles from the ground. Many years ago a resort here trapped the water in bathing tanks, all long since removed.

For the next mile the path continues above the Ohanapecosh River, passes a spur trail to the right, and then drops sharply to the left across a bridge and a head-on view of the Silver Falls. To appreciate the entire torrent, continue across the bridge, following paths to the right along the bluff above the falls.

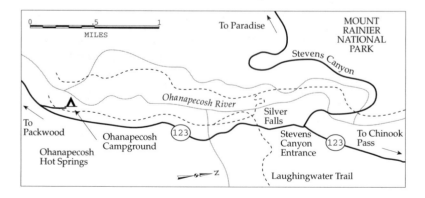

Ohanapecosh River near campground

Return here either the way you came or by a trail on the other side of the river that climbs above and away from the river though forest back to the campground again.

The falls can also be reached from the Stevens Canyon Road across from the rest room west of the entrance station. This path travels down above the river, dropping alongside the falls to the bridge in about ½ mile.

Grove of the Patriarchs

64 Grove of the Patriarchs

Features: giant trees
One way: ¾ mile
Elevation gain: slight
Difficulty: easy
Open: spring through fall
Map: Green Trails 270

Elegant! Truly elegant! Grand and beautiful trees, some 1,000 years old, on a soggy island surrounded by the Ohanapecosh River.

From Enumclaw or Yakima take Highway 410 to Cayuse Pass, driving south 12 miles on Highway 123 to the Stevens Canyon entrance to Mount Rainier National Park.

Find the trail behind the rest room just beyond the entrance station. The path drops down above the Ohanapecosh River and forks to the right in about ½ mile across a footbridge to a forest loop.

Don't hurry here. It took these trees centuries and centuries to grow. They deserve more than a moment's admiration.

Paths lead past most of the grand trees here: a cedar more than 25 feet in circumference. A Douglas fir more than 38 feet around. With places now and then to sit and listen to the giants groan in the wind.

The flat here is flooded periodically by high water in the spring, forcing changes some years in the trail. But the old giants simply wait (or is it wade?) it out.

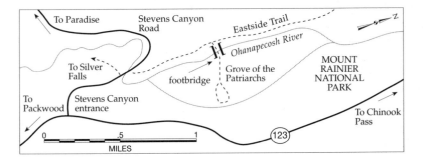

 65 Round Mountain

Features: forest, lookout vistas
One way: 2½ miles
Elevation gain: 270 feet
Difficulty: steep to steeper
Open: summer
Maps: Green Trails 303; Goat Rocks Wilderness

The only east-side view in this book of the Goat Rocks, White Pass, Mount Rainier, and Mount Adams. With Clear and Rimrock lakes at your feet. Although you may wonder as you hike why it is you came.

From Enumclaw or Randle drive to White Pass on Highway 12, turning right onto Clear Lake Road (also called Road 12) in about 7.5 miles east of the pass.

From Yakima follow White Pass Highway 12 beyond Rimrock Lake, turning left on Clear Lake Road 12 at Clear Lake.

From Clear Lake Road 12, turn right in 3 miles to Road 830, finding the trailhead at the end of the road.

The path starts up an abandoned mining road, enters the Goat Rocks Wilderness, and then forks to the right at a barricade on the mine road to an old trail marked by blazes.

Shortly the trail climbs steeply up a series of switchbacks across loose scree to more open and steeper slopes. The trail enters trees (walk left to the edge of a ridge that looks down on Dog

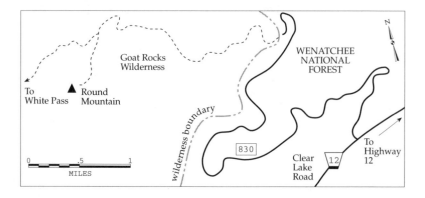

Clear Lake (right) *and Rimrock Lake (reservoir) from Round Mountain*

Lake) and finally to a trail marked by a cairn that leads to the left and climbs from steep to very steep to the old lookout site.

Take a forest map to identify the lakes, ridges, and mountains here and to give names to Old Snowy, Ives, and Gilbert peaks along the Goat Rocks. All from the stone doorsteps—all that's left—of the old lookout. At 5,970 feet. Carry water. And a lunch.

Castle Butte and Mount Rainier from Cispus Point

 Cispus Point

Features: lake, vistas
One way: 2½ miles or less
Elevation gain: 1,100 feet
Difficulty: moderate to very steep
Open: summer
Maps: Green Trails 302, 334

Follow a section of the high old Klickitat Trail No. 7, established by Indians, no one knows how long ago, along this ridge between the Cowlitz and Cispus rivers, to a spur trail built for fire patrols that leads to the top of Cispus Point.

On Highway 12, drive 12.8 miles east of Randle or about 3.5 miles southwest of Packwood, turning east on Smith Creek Road (also called Road 20) and driving 12 miles to a Klickitat Trail sign. Or another 0.7 mile to an unmarked logging spur on the left.

From the Klickitat sign, follow an old logging spur around the right side of an old clear-cut to a signed trail in about 100 yards. The path drops past a soggy meadow (watch for elk) to the outlet of Jackpot Lake. Beyond the lake, the trail climbs through forest, then follows colored posts and plastic tag lines across still more clear-cuts to a sign that says "TRAIL."

If you start your hike on the unmarked logging spur farther up Road 20, follow the spur left until it too comes to the sign.

From the sign, the trail starts uphill steeply through rock gardens and waist-high shrubs, first to a trail junction (turn left) and then on to the top of Cispus Point at 5,656 feet.

Tarns near the top afford a moment of level trail before the end with its views down on Randle, toward Castle Butte, and out at Mount Rainier, Mount Adams, the Goat Rocks, and anything else you can locate on your forest map.

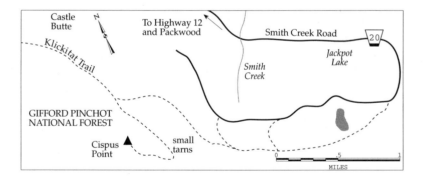

 Hamilton Butte

Features: vistas, high meadows
One way: 1½ miles
Elevation gain: 900 feet
Difficulty: steep
Open: summer
Map: Green Trails 334

Spend an hour, an afternoon, or a night—if you lug a pack—
on a small patch of meadow atop a mountain butte only one step
from the stars.

Still heavenly despite the insults of Mount St. Helens and
the terrible damage done to those recovering slopes by fools on
raging, noisy motorbikes encouraged, yet, by the Forest Service.

In Randle turn south off Highway 12, cross the Cowlitz
River, turning left in about 1 mile onto Road 23. In about 11.5
miles turn left on Road 22, the North Fork road, continuing another 5.8 miles to turn right on Road 78.

Follow Road 78 uphill about 7.5 miles, turning left on Road
7807 (marked "HAMILTON BUTTE TRAIL 2 MILES"). Find the trail at
the end of a steep spur road beyond Mud Lake. Do *not* drive beyond the blocked parking area. The road has been trenched. No
turnaround.

The path continues up the blocked road, giving way to a trail
beyond a junction with a rutted road/trail to the right. From here

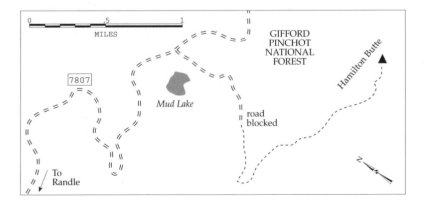

Mount Rainier above motorcycle ruts in Hamilton Butte Trail

on follow motorbike ruts of your choice to the top of the butte at 5,772 feet. Cliffs to look over, rock points to pose on, and slabs to nap against.

This entire area was buried in pumice when Mount St. Helens erupted. Plants—those that have escaped the ravages of motorbikes—only now are beginning their struggle to reclaim this once grassy and flowered knob. Scientists are even watching recovery of the small mud lake, once populated with salamanders.

Thankfully, the vistas remain—Wobbly Lake, Rainier, Adams, the Goat Rocks, a hint of Hood, and what's left of St. Helens—despite the blotches of clear-cuts and scars left by the ruthless trail machines. A carnage permitted on most trails here by the Forest Service that encourages continued expansion of their use.

 Tongue Mountain

Features: plunging vistas
One way: 2 miles
Elevation gain: 1,200 feet
Difficulty: moderate to very steep
Open: midsummer
Map: Green Trails 333

No bad dream this: it's real. The trail ends at the very edge of a 3,300-foot cliff! With a fantastic view, what else.

In Randle turn south off Highway 12, cross the Cowlitz River, turning left in about 1 mile onto Road 23, turning right onto Road 29 in about 8 miles and then left in another mile after crossing the Cispus River. In 4 miles turn left on Road 2904, driving to the crest of Juniper Ridge in another 4 miles.

At the ridge, take the trail north, first losing elevation and then gaining it again through scraggly forest for about 1¼ miles to an unmarked trail to the right uphill (just as the main trail starts generally downhill.)

The path to the mountain top climbs sharply to open meadows—lots of flowers in season—and then zigzags gracefully, safely, and persistently across open slopes to a cleft between two rock peaks. (The path here, although not heavily used, is fairly well marked by St. Helens pumice.)

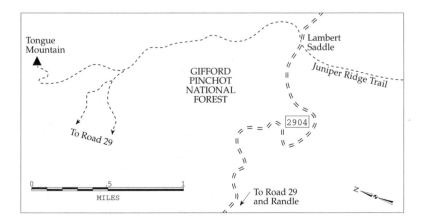

Don't rush the last few feet. The trail ends abruptly at the edge of a cliff with a breathtaking drop straight down into the Cispus River.

Big views of Mount Rainier, St. Helens, and Adams from the cleft. The trail that once led to the lookout, higher yet, slid out years ago leaving bare rock. Best to stop at the cleft.

Phlox on Tongue Mountain

Camp Creek Falls

69 Camp Creek Falls

Features: waterfall
One way: ⅓ mile
Elevation gain: slight
Difficulty: easy to moderate
Open: summer
Map: Green Trails 333

Grandeur here? Hardly. Spectacle? A quiet one perhaps.

Peace? Oh, yes. In fact, you may be the only visitor to this special place.

In Randle turn south off Highway 12, cross the Cowlitz River, turning left in about 1 mile onto Road 23, continuing about 9.6 miles (just beyond the junction with Road 29). If you cross Camp Creek you've gone 50 yards too far.

Find the trail from the road into trees to the left. A small parking area on the right.

The trail here starts through pleasant open forest of big trees and forest flowers. (You won't notice the creek at all.) In a long ¼ mile, at a junction with an abandoned trail, turn right and follow the path, climbing now, to a point where it turns sharply left.

And surprise! A 30-foot waterfall that looks more like 50. With a trail along a steep side slope that brings it face to face.

It's a collector's item, truly. One of those rare, small waterfalls that looks and sounds like a perfect waterfall should.

The abandoned main trail continues up a ridge into logging country.

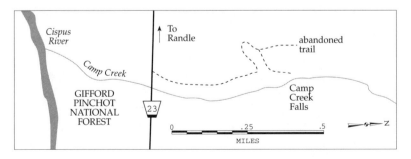

70 North Fork Loop

Features: forest, vistas
One way: 1½-mile loop
Elevation gain: 400 feet
Difficulty: steep to moderate
Open: summer
Map: Green Trails 333

Hike from a forested campground to a forested plateau with views over the Cispus Valley, up at Juniper Ridge, and the face of towering Tongue Mountain (hike 68).

In Randle turn south off Highway 12, cross the Cowlitz River, and turn left in about 1 mile onto Road 23, driving on to the North Fork Campground on the left side of the road in about 12 more miles.

Park at the end of the campground loop near the old North Fork Guard Station (if there's room). Hikers can be charged a camp fee if they park in any of the campsites while hiking. Find the trail uphill, to the right, beside the North Fork Guard Station.

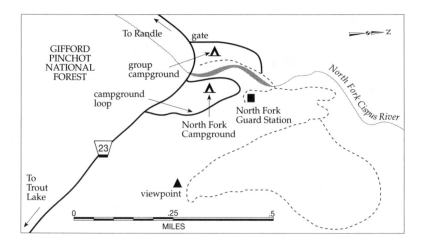

Tongue Mountain from North Fork Loop trail

The trail switchbacks sharply to the top of the plateau and a stand of grand old-growth Douglas fir and hemlock, almost too tall to look up to.

Bear to the right at the top and follow the path around the edge of the plateau. Spur paths lead to views from the edge of an overhanging cliff down on the valley and out at the mountains. Not for uncontrolled children.

The path continues through forest and along the edge of a clear-cut before dropping back to the campground and bridge.

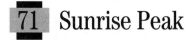 Sunrise Peak

Features: meadows, vistas
One way: 1¼–3 miles
Elevation gain: 1,600 feet
Difficulty: moderate to very steep
Open: late summer
Maps: Green Trails 333, 334

Climb through enchanting meadows to a spectacle of distant peaks from an abandoned lookout site at 5,892 feet.

In Randle turn south off Highway 12, cross the Cowlitz River, and turn left in about 1 mile onto Road 23, following it beyond North Fork Campground (see hike 70, North Fork Loop), bearing right across the Cispus River, still on Road 23, at a junction with Road 21. In about 5 more miles turn right (east) onto Road 2324. Find the trailhead in another 5 miles off Road 2324 on logging spur Road 063.

The path climbs quickly and sharply to meadows in about ½ mile with views of Rainier, Adams, and Hood.

Two choices now: take a longer hike straight ahead across meadows toward Jumbo Peak, turning right at a junction with the Juniper Ridge trail, heavily rutted by uncontrolled motorbikes. Then, after a long ¾ mile, climb to the right up switchbacks to the old lookout site.

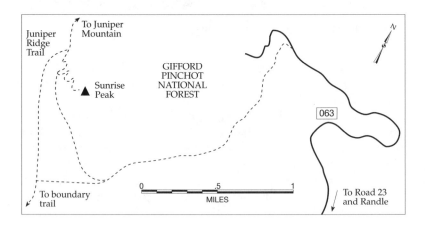

Or, climb a steeper, fainter, sometimes unsigned but less damaged trail to the right about ¼ mile after you crest the meadow plateau. This path, across a steep meadow, offers a shorter lurch to the lookout.

Enjoy easy views from a ledge where the trail ends or climb— with care—to the lookout site atop rocks to vistas that now include Rainier, Adams, Hood, and St. Helens's gaping crater.

Mount Rainier from Sunrise Peak

Mount Adams from Takhlakh Lake

 72 Takh Takh Meadow

Features: ponds, meadows, lava flows
One way: 1½-mile loop
Elevation gain: 200 feet
Difficulty: moderate
Open: midsummer
Map: Green Trails 334 (trail not shown)

From one of the most spectacular mountain lakes in the state (Mount Adams's reflection fills all of it), hike to marshy ponds filled with marshy flowers and then up to the top of arid volcanic lava flows.

Lots of bugs in the spring and summer. Best in the fall.

In Randle turn south off Highway 12 and cross the Cowlitz River. Turn left in about 1 mile onto Road 23, turning left again in about 33 miles—at the crest of the ridge, 0.5 mile short of Baby Shoe Pass—onto Road 2329. To Takhlakh Lake and Campground. Find the trail along the lake below the campground.

Follow the lakeshore trail to the right, continuing straight ahead at a fork in the trail at the end of the lake. At a second trail junction, turn right and hike through forest to Road 2329.

Cross the road to a pond and explore a short way-trail to the right along the edge of the pond through bear grass, lupine, gentians, bog orchids, and elephant head flowers—each in its season—before returning to pick up the main trail to the left.

The main path continues to another pond and then climbs the frozen, furrowed snout of a lava flow to thin forest—even heather now—and then back to the road and the loop trail that returns to the lake.

Trees in this subalpine area include mountain hemlock, noble, alpine, and silver firs, and white and lodgepole pines. In soggy areas near the ponds at the base of the lava flows, trees range up to 200 years old.

If you camp at the lake, walk the trail around the shore. Pleasant any time of day. About 1 mile.

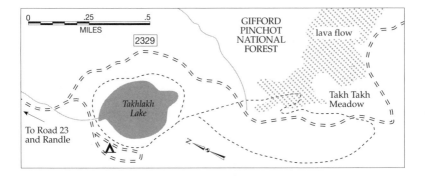

 Council Bluff

Features: lake, views
One way: 1½ miles
Elevation gain: 1,000 feet
Difficulty: steep
Open: summer
Map: Green Trails 334

Hike from a mountain lake to a former lookout site within arm's reach of Mount Adams—or so it seems.

In Randle turn south off Highway 12, cross the Cowlitz River, and turn left in about 1 mile onto Road 23, driving on to Baby Shoe Pass in about 33 miles. At the pass, follow Road 23 to the right, turning right again in about 1.5 miles onto Road 2334, following signs to Council Lake.

Find the path off the far side of the Council Lake Campground up sharply on a sometimes-closed-and-sometimes-open but always unmaintained road. Follow the road about 1¼ miles to a small parking spot. Climb a trail to the right the last 500 feet to the top of the bluff at 5,180 feet in ⅓ mile.

Explore paths around the bluff or just stand in awe of Adams just across the way, Council Lake at your feet, with Rainier and other Cascade peaks in a grand chorus around them.

Not a place to hurry from. In fact, it seems to beg you to stay for one more look and one more dream for just one more time.

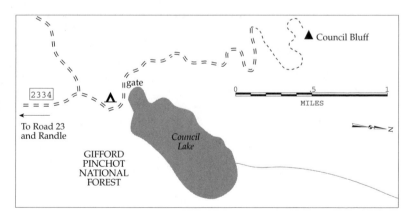

Council Lake and Mount Adams from Council Bluff

74 Iron Creek Campground Loop

Features: river, great trees
One way: 1½ miles
Elevation gain: none
Difficulty: easy
Open: spring through fall
Map: Green Trails 333

This is without doubt the easiest wander—not hike—in this book. And it's also one of the most beautiful with a gorgeous river and magnificent trees that demand to be loved and admired.

From Randle, turn south to Road 25, driving to its junction with Road 76 and the entrance to the Iron Creek Campground. The trail loops the campground and can be accessed from camps along the Cispus River or from the campground picnic area.

The best walk here is the stretch between the campsites and the river. Huge Douglas firs tower to the sky and lovely cathedral groves of cedars urge whispers as you walk.

And all this with flowers, lush ferns, huckleberries, devil's club, and feasts of fat yellow salmonberries in the spring. Even giants sprawled out on the forest floor (some, you'll note, were cut down) look as grand in death as they did alive. Walk their length, admire the mysteries of their growth, and wonder why the few were cut down.

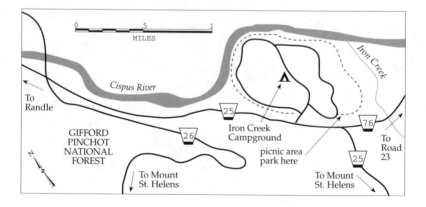

Interpretive sign at beginning of campground trail

No need to hurry here. No need to work or strain. Stroll only. Listening, looking, noting every detail of the beauty that surrounds you. Pleasant even in the rain. Spectacular in the fog.

 Burley Mountain

Features: lookout, vistas
One way: ½ mile
Elevation gain: about 500 feet
Difficulty: moderately steep
Open: late summer
Map: Green Trails 333

Climb a huckleberry ridge to a manned lookout, one of the three out of sixty left in the Gifford Pinchot National Forest, watched over by all three great sentinel peaks in these South Cascades.

Drive south from Randle on Road 25, turning left on Road 76 beyond the entrance to Iron Creek Campground. In 4.4 miles from the campground, turn south (right) onto Road 77.

The narrow dirt road climbs through forest to a four-way junction at the top of a ridge in 7.6 miles. Turn left on narrow Road 7605, driving another 1.5 miles to Spur Road 086 and a parking area directly below the lookout.

Walk the final switchback up the road to the lookout at 5,304 feet on an alpine ridge heavily doused with pumice from Mount St. Helens.

Rainier, Adams, and St. Helens, joined by the Goat Rocks, Hood, and other Cascade peaks both north and south, circle this solitary point in the sky. Above blotch after blotch of clear-cuts.

Lots and lots of huckleberries in the fall on slopes below the lookout.

Check at the ranger station in Randle before you start your trip if visiting with a resident, working lookout is important to you.

Mount Rainier, and family picking blueberries near Burley Mountain

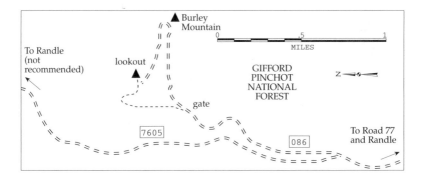

Mount St. Helens and blast area from top of Strawberry Mountain

76 Strawberry Mountain

Features: views of Mount St. Helens's destruction
One way: ¾ mile or more
Elevation gain: 500 feet
Difficulty: steep
Open: summer
Map: Green Trails 332

Hike along the edge of Mount St. Helens's violence to awesome views of the volcano's damage from an abandoned lookout site at 5,464 feet.

From Randle drive south on Road 25 about 17 miles, turning right on Road 2516, following it about 6 miles to the crest of the Strawberry Mountain divide. (The road continues down the other side of the divide to a "viewpoint" in about 1 mile.)

The trail from the parking area at the crest of the road starts up an old logging track to the left, turning uphill to the right into undamaged forest in about ¼ mile, there to climb after several leaps and bounds to a saddle and junction on the edge of the ridge. Note how the slope facing St. Helens has been blasted bare while forest just over the ridge stands untouched.

Take the uphill path to the right (the trail left follows the ridge top to the Boundary Trail) first to a radio repeater station in a leveled clearing and then by trail off the end of the repeater station clearing on to the lookout site.

At the top pause and wonder. All of the great peaks—Rainier, St. Helens, Hood—stand around you in the distance but the wonders lie at your feet. Note how the 1980 blast laid the forest flat as though swept by some giant comb in most places, just clipped the tops off trees in some, and spared trees entirely in others.

Remembering that not all of the damage you see was suffered in the eruption. Some of the squalor around barren Ryan Lake below you was caused by logging before the eruption, and some of it in the valley was caused by logging afterward.

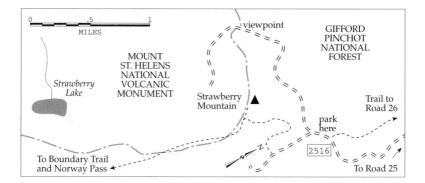

 Norway Pass

Features: blast damage, recovery, Mount St. Helens
One way: 2½ miles
Elevation gain: 900 feet
Difficulty: moderate to steep
Open: midsummer
Map: Visitors Guide to Mount St. Helens National Volcanic
  Monument

Walk through the enormity of a blast that literally combed these mountain forests flat to a view of the massive lava dome from which all this power leapt.

From Randle drive south some 20 miles on Road 25 to Road 99, turning right into the Mount St. Helens National Volcanic Monument. In 9 miles turn right again onto Road 26, continuing beyond Meta Lake, and finding the Norway Pass trail parking area on the left.

The path starts out through a massive snarl of toppled trees and climbs a slope, first to the left above Meta Lake and then to the right to a saddle with a sweeping view of destruction to the north.

The path then drops through an area protected from the blast (but not the falling cloud of pumice), crosses a creek, and then climbs on to Norway Pass.

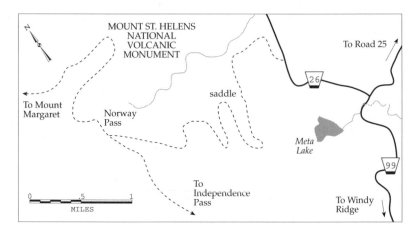

Views of Mount Adams and Mount Rainier are joined at the pass by a head-on view to the south into St. Helens's crater at the far end of Spirit Lake.

With other surprises of reality all along the way:

With paintbrush, penstemon, and avalanche lilies—sometimes as many as nine blossoms to a stem—growing along a protected creek as though nothing had happened around them at all. With pumice that flowed almost like water to form deltas in basins at the bottom of decimated slopes. With giant trees stretched out like corpses side by side. With other trees, like frozen dancers, poised still where they were thrown. With silence, utter silence, where nothing grows. And in every secure corner, new green plants rising from the pumice. Huckleberries. Trees. Even birds. With grass, as Carl Sandburg said, with grass that covers all.

Mount St. Helens and Spirit Lake from Norway Pass prior to 1980 eruption (compare to present view from Independence Pass, page 177)

78 Independence Pass

Features: St. Helens's crater, Spirit Lake
One way: 1½ miles
Elevation gain: about 500 feet
Difficulty: moderate to steep
Open: midsummer
Map: Green Trails 332

Hike up and then down through trees stripped to the bone, tossed like jackstraws and then buried in pumice. Above once-forested slopes scoured by a tidal wave and a lake covered with the wave's log debris. To a view into the maw of the volcano that did it all.

From Randle drive south some 20 miles on Road 25 to Road 99, turning right into the Mount St. Helens National Volcanic Monument, driving 12-plus miles to the signed Independence Pass trailhead on the right.

The trail starts up stairsteps from a parking area and then climbs ¼ mile to a viewpoint. Continue past the viewpoint for 1½ miles as the trail switchbacks upward and then traverses across the side of a blasted slope before dropping to cross a sometime stream.

Beyond the stream, the trail climbs around the shoulder of a ridge to a spit of rock that juts out above the lake to the left be-

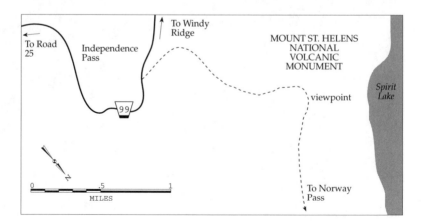

*Spirit Lake and Mount St. Helens from Independence Pass Trail
(compare to photo on page 175)*

low the trail. A way path leads over rocks and debris to a limited
viewing area perched on the spit of cliffs. No place here for children or skittish adults. Similar views also from the trail.

To the south, note St. Helens's crater and the huge raft of
logs that covers almost half of Spirit Lake. The logs were ripped
from the shore (note the barren slopes) by the tidal wave produced when the side of St. Helens collapsed into Spirit Lake.

The destruction here, however, only hints at the violence of
the eruption. In the big eruption on May 18, 1980, winds reached
almost the speed of sound. Temperatures soared to more than
600 degrees Fahrenheit in an explosion equal to a twenty-four-
megaton atom bomb. With half the mass of the blast disgorged in
less than 20 seconds, triggering a landslide of almost two cubic
miles of rock, earth, and ice. Destroying, uprooting, and hurling
trees, boulders, and huge blocks of ice over more than 300 square
miles north of the mountain.

And most surprising: in utter silence. Witnesses saw the
blast but, despite the destruction, heard nothing at all.

To the north of the rock spit, look up at Norway Pass (hike
77) where your trail ends steeply in another 1¾ miles. And below, to the south, note the Harmony Falls trail as it drops to the
lake (hike 79).

Return the way you came.

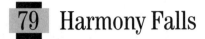 Harmony Falls

Features: blast and tidal wave areas, Spirit Lake
One way: 1 mile
Elevation gain: about 700 feet
Difficulty: steep
Open: midsummer
Map: Green Trails 332

Imagine: A lodge tucked below great trees above a crystal lake with a 60-foot waterfall tumbling from Harmony Creek nearby. And a glorious and perfect cone-shaped Mount St. Helens overlooking it all.

Mount St. Helens pumice

Then see the reality of what that perfect mountain did in 1980 in a gargantuan blast that blew 1,300 feet off the top of the peak, sent a cloud of debris 15 miles into the air, toppled 230 square miles of forest, dumped ash over more than 22,000 square miles, and emitted a stream of dust that circled the earth.

From Randle drive south some 20 miles on Road 25 to Road 99, turning right into the Mount St. Helens National Volcanic Monument, finding the signed Harmony viewpoint to the right in about 12.5 miles. No hiking off trails in this restricted area.

The trail drops sharply through blasted forest into an area swept of trees in a tidal wave created when the side of the mountain plunged into the lake, causing a catastrophic wave 850 feet high and raising the level of the lake almost 200 feet. Scientists estimate that up to two cubic *miles* of earth blew out of the side of the mountain, most of it into the lake, in the largest May 18, 1980, eruption.

The trail ends on a barren sand plateau at the edge of the re-formed Spirit Lake near Harmony Creek. The creek still flows into the lake but only a hint of Harmony Falls remains. All evidence of the lodge was obliterated in the blast.

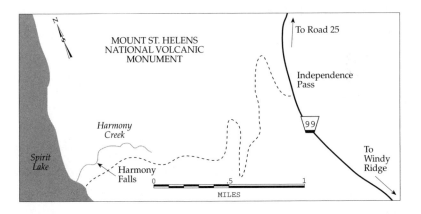

Barrier-free trail around tree casts

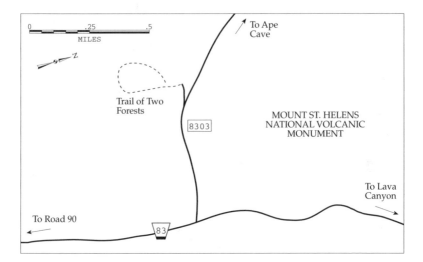

80 Trail of Two Forests

Features: a new forest, lava molds of an ancient one
One way: ¼ mile
Elevation gain: none
Difficulty: moderate
Open: summer
Map: Visitors Guide to Mount St. Helens National Volcanic
Monument

So short a trail leads to so unusual a scene: A new forest growing out of old lava rock that contains molds of a forest captured in molten lava more than 2,000 years ago.

From I-5, drive east from Exit 21 at Woodland to Highway 503, driving 29 miles past Lake Merwin to Cougar on Road 90 and about 7 more miles to Road 83.

Or from Randle, drive 45 miles south on Road 25 to Road 90, turning right and driving to the west end of Swift Reservoir to Road 83.

On Road 83 drive north 3 miles to Road 8303 and the unusual Two Forests lava/tree display.

Find the trail through this large sampling of tree molds beyond the parking area near the rest room. The boardwalk trail permits an easy walk through the rough lava to fine samplings of the tree casts, some broken open, others still standing intact, others sprawled on the ground. Note the fine details of bark captured in many of the casts.

The showpiece of the trail is a large cast that visitors (children in particular) are invited to crawl through and see an ancient tree from the inside out.

(The casts here are only a sample of others to be found nearby and in other lava fields around Mount St. Helens. Finding the others, however, can be difficult and risky. Travel through these fields of rough lava without a path can be difficult and the casts sometimes lie hidden under brush.)

 Ape Cave

Features: lower and upper lava caves
One way: lower cave, less than ½ mile; upper cave, less than 1½
 miles
Elevation gain: slight
Difficulty: lights required, rough and narrow sections
Open: year-round
Map: Visitors Guide to Mount St. Helens National Volcanic
 Monument

Walk down steps and ladders into the cool, dark bowels of the longest intact lava tube cave in the continental United States, and then through huge rooms and small openings, over rubble, and beneath a huge lava "meatball" stuck in the ceiling of the cave.

This and other caves like it were formed when molten lava, moving downhill, cooled and congealed on the outside while the remaining liquid inside continued to move, leaving a tube.

From I-5, drive east from Exit 21 at Woodland to Highway 503, driving 29 miles past Lake Merwin to Cougar on Road 90, and about 7 more miles to Road 83.

From Randle, drive 45 miles south on Road 25 to Road 90, turning right and driving to the west end of Swift Reservoir to Road 83.

On Road 83 drive north 3 miles, turning left to Road 8303, reaching the cave in little more than a mile.

Enter the cave from the visitor center parking area. Walk first down concrete steps to the main entrance level and then down a metal stairway into the main cave.

Hikes into a lower cave, which slopes about 4,000 feet downhill from the entrance stairway, offer the easiest walk and

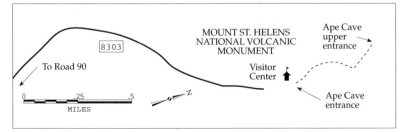

Ape Cave's "meatball"

feature the much-photographed lava ball (meatball) wedged into the ceiling of the cave. Less than ½ mile from the entrance.

The upper cave, which slopes uphill, passes through the cave's largest room in more than 100 yards. Beyond the room, the way through the uphill cave leads through a good deal of collapsed rock before reaching an exit in less than 1½ miles. All, of course, except for the light you carry, in total darkness.

With several warnings: There are no lights in the cave at all. You must carry your own. Recommended are three light sources per person. Gas lanterns can be rented at the cave headquarters.

In addition, wear warm clothes and sturdy shoes plus a hard hat if you plan extensive explorations. The temperature in the cave is 42 degrees Fahrenheit and explorations may require climbing over sharp and rough lava and through small openings.

Formal guided lantern walks are offered from the cave headquarters during the summer.

 Lava Canyon

Features: scoured canyon
One way: ½ mile or more
Elevation gain: slight
Difficulty: steep grades, cliffs
Open: midsummer
Map: Visitors Guide to Mount St. Helens National Volcanic
   Monument

Surreal truly: an eerie, barren gorge of small waterfalls gouged out by mudflows cascading from melted glaciers higher on St. Helens.

From I-5, drive east from Exit 21 at Woodland to Highway 503, driving 29 miles past Lake Merwin to Cougar on Road 90 and about 7 more miles to Road 83.

From Randle, drive 45 miles south on Road 25 to Road 90, turning right and driving to the west end of Swift Reservoir to Road 83.

On Road 83 drive north 11 miles to a parking area at the end of the road.

Find a loop trail downhill off the right side of the parking area. The path starts out in trees but quickly drops into the heavily eroded Muddy River Gorge gouged out when the eruption of Mount St. Helens plunged something like 3.5 billion gallons of water, mud, and debris, in one violent slug, down the Muddy and nearby Pine rivers. Enough to cover 11,000 acres with a foot of water and debris.

The loop leads first to a junction at a bridge across the river.

The path to the right crosses the river above a small waterfall and then continues to the left around and over large outcrops

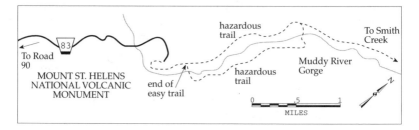

of lava that survived the eroding flood. Way paths lead to views atop the outcrops into the river canyon. The path loops back across the river in about 1 mile at a suspension bridge.

Back at the junction, the path straight ahead continues down the left side of the river with warnings about narrow trails across cliff faces and steep grades. The last formal viewpoint at the end of a switchback—with warnings again—permits views down on small waterfalls in the canyon.

Stop here if the trail ahead spooks you as it drops across the face of a cliff. Continue on if it doesn't (it's safe) to the suspension bridge and the return trail on the other side of the river.

Waterfall in Lava Canyon

Cedar Flats Research Natural Area

 Cedar Flats

Features: enchanted forest
One way: 1-mile loop
Elevation gain: level
Difficulty: easy
Open: summer
Maps: Green Trails 364; Visitors Guide to Mount St. Helens
National Volcanic Monument

A truly enchanted forest. Surrounded by clear-cuts. Wounded
by the raging Muddy River when Mount St. Helens erupted.
Still raged at by streams of logging trucks. Opening its shroud

of beauty now only to those who come asking to understand. A protected Natural Area.

From I-5 Exit 21 at Woodland drive east 23 miles on Highway 503 and, after 503 turns south, another 24 miles on Road 90 to its junction with Road 25 from Randle. Turn left onto Road 25 and find the small entrance trail into this awesome forest from a small parking spot on the right in 3.7 miles.

Or from Randle, drive south about 41.3 miles on Road 25 to the trailhead on the left.

The path drops behind a rail fence into a grove of great cedars and Douglas fir, crosses a creek, loops to the right into the richest corner of forest described in this book or to be found, perhaps, anywhere in the western Cascades.

No signs here at all. You'll understand only what you take time to see. Finding answers in every case that will outweigh the questions you ask. For the grandeur here at every turn speaks for itself. In cathedral groves. Arbors of maple. Amid flowered root-fans of giants who died. And sturdy young trees waiting for surviving giants to fall. With corners of devil's club and salmonberry defying them all.

The trail leaves the forest only once, breaking out over the barren floodplain of the Muddy River where the deluge triggered by St. Helens's mighty belch ripped this corner of the forest away.

Walk here with expectations and leave with more knowledge of yourself and nature than you ever expected to find.

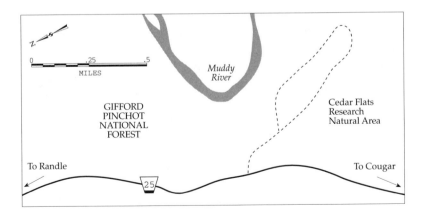

 Curly Creek Falls

Features: a rock arch etched by a waterfall
One way: up to ¾ mile
Elevation gain: slight
Difficulty: easy
Open: summer
Map: Visitors Guide to Mount St. Helens National Volcanic
Monument

Take a short hike here to see an eroded arch in the middle of
a frenzied little stairstep waterfall on Curly Creek just across
and above the Lewis River. And then walk a little farther to see
how a falls on Miller Creek manages to enjoy a simpler, more
straightforward splash.

From I-5 Exit 21 at Woodland, drive east on Highway 503
and then Road 90 to Cougar, continuing 4.3 miles beyond the
junction with Road 25 (from Randle), turning left to Road 9039
and the Lewis River bridge.

Or from Randle, drive about 45 miles on Road 25 to Road 90,
turning left in about 4.3 miles to Road 9039 and the Lewis River
bridge.

Find the trail to the left of Road 9039 just beyond the bridge.

The path drops through overhanging vine maples to make its
way above the river to a formal viewpoint of Curly Creek Falls

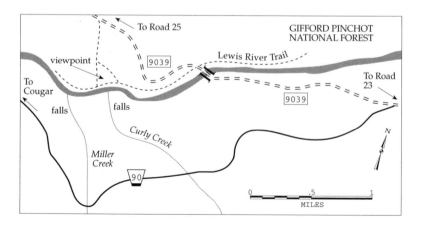

Curly Creek Falls

and its grated rock arches across the river. The arches themselves were etched with holes before the water formed the arch.

To view Miller Creek Falls across the river on Miller Creek (without an arch), walk another ¼ mile.

For an easier but less interesting way to the falls, drive up-hill about 0.25 mile beyond the bridge over the Lewis River to a formal parking area on the left. A shorter path leads to the view-point but lacks the presence of the river. The falls sometimes dries up in late autumn.

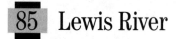 Lewis River

Features: forest, river
One way: up to or less than 2¼ miles
Elevation gain: slight
Difficulty: easy
Open: summer
Map: Green Trails 365

A quiet trail along the Lewis River goes just about as far as you want to walk it. With one warning: mountain bikers on weekends may run you off the trail. Bolt Shelter in 2.2 miles.

From I-5 Exit 21 at Woodland, drive east on Highway 503 and then Road 90 to Cougar, turning left in 4.3 miles to Road 9039 to cross the bridge over the Lewis River.

Or from Randle, drive about 45 miles on Road 25 to Road 90, turning left another 4.3 miles to Road 9039 and the bridge over the Lewis River.

Find the trail off the right of Road 9039 just beyond the bridge.

The path starts above this untamed stretch of river through pleasant, mature forest with lovely Douglas fir and makes its way with modest ups and downs above a string of rapids.

No flower meadows here but a full display of mountain forest flowers and ferns with everything from queen's cups through pipsissewas, Oregon grape, and foam flowers with sword, maidenhair, and licorice ferns in between. Bring your flower book. Pieces of petrified wood are sometimes found along the river.

Rest spots along the way for daydreaming as you listen to the river argue with itself.

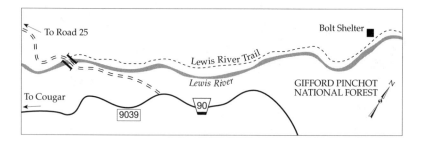

Lewis River Trail

Cotton grass in Spencer Meadow

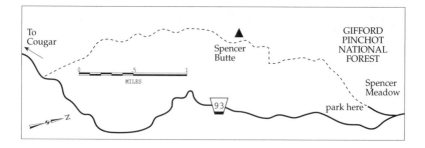

86 Spencer Butte

Features: forest, views
One way: 1½ miles
Elevation gain: 650 feet
Difficulty: steep
Open: midsummer
Map: Green Trails 365

Quiet, clear views of Mount St. Helens over a soggy meadow filled with cotton grass. And then, from the top of 4,247-foot Spencer Butte, add Mounts Rainier, Hood, and Jefferson.

From I-5 Exit 21 at Woodland, drive 29 miles east on Highway 503 and Road 90 to Cougar, and another 18 miles to the junction with Road 25 from Randle. Turn toward Randle on Road 25 and then right in 5 miles to Road 93.

Or from Randle, drive about 41 miles on Road 25, turning left to Road 93.

On Road 93 drive about 12 miles to Spencer Meadow and the trailhead to Spencer Butte, at the end of a short spur road to the left. (Ignore the first Spencer Butte sign you see along the road. The trail from Spencer Meadow is more interesting.)

At the meadow (an undeveloped road leads to the left to a pretty clearing), prowl its edges for bog-type flowers, watching too for elk and deer.

The trail to the top of the butte starts to the left off the entrance spur at the end of a four-wheel-drive track and climbs steeply uphill to a path heavily used by motorbikes and elk.

No switchbacks. The trail climbs one long traverse steadily, as the mountain climbs, through meadows surrounded by patches of Douglas fir and white pine. Views of Mount Adams to your left and St. Helens to the right.

The trail becomes a motorbike rut—not even the elk can walk in it—as it climbs huckleberry slopes before ending at the old lookout site. Find vistas through the trees or from a bigger meadow a few yards beyond the lookout site.

Return the way you came or, if you can arrange to be picked up, follow the trail beyond the high meadow back to the trail sign you passed on Road 93 driving up.

87 Lower and Middle Lewis River Falls

Features: great and little waterfalls
One way: 1¼ miles or more
Elevation gain: 200 feet
Difficulty: easy
Open: summer
Map: Green Trails 365

A little photogenic falls on Copper Creek and two grand waterfalls on the Lewis River—all in one big package from one very pleasant campground in very lovely forest.

From I-5 Exit 21 at Woodland, drive 47 miles east on Highway 503 and Road 90 through Cougar to the junction with Road 25 from Randle, continuing 14.2 miles on Road 90 to the Lower Falls Campground on the right.

Or, from Randle drive 50 miles south on Road 25 to Road 90, turning left onto Road 90 and continuing 14.2 miles to the campground (see above).

Or, from the high country around Takhlakh Lake, drive from Road 23 west 16.5 miles on Road 90 to the campground.

Starting from the campground, walk toward the river, turning left on a trail to Middle Falls in 1¼ miles. The path travels through a forest of old white-splotched fir on a flat that once was probably the bed of the river now rushing far below.

In about ½ mile, note part of a bridge perched in the middle of the river. The bridge near a small campground on the other side of the river was built but never completed as part of a logging road that was to access the forests on the north (your) side of the river.

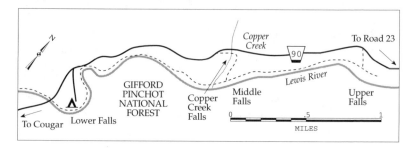

Middle Lewis River Falls

In about a mile the trail drops below a towering moss cliff dripping with monkey flowers and maidenhair ferns to cross Copper Creek below the small, photogenic waterfall tumbling over a series of rock slabs.

The path continues to the base of Middle Falls which spans the river with water plunging freely in one section and washing over tiers of rock in another. With water ouzels, naturally.

(The Middle Falls can also be reached down a steep ¼-mile trail from Road 90 about ½ mile east of the campground.)

See the Lower Lewis River Falls as you return to the campground by following the river trail downstream to a viewpoint above the falls or to a stairway leading down to places near it.

The water on this falls, located at a point where the river makes a turn, can't decide which way to go. A U-shaped snout of rock extends downstream with water streaming over it in all directions.

The trail continues downstream along a series of railed viewpoints before making its way farther downriver.

Coldwater Lake and Mount St. Helens

88 Johnston Ridge

Features: vistas, lake
One way: ¼–2 miles
Elevation gain: substantial
Difficulty: moderate to very steep
Open: summer
Map: Visitors Guide to Mount St. Helens National Volcanic
Monument

Hike across logged and blasted slopes, along an instant lake,
and atop high, barren ridges to views deep into Mount St. Helens's
gaping maw.

(Note: Some of the features listed here were still being developed as this was written. Others, not mentioned, were being
planned. The U.S. Forest Service regulations forbid travel off
trails anywhere in this area.)

From I-5 Exit 60 to Toledo and Highway 505, or from Exit 49
at Castle Rock to Highway 504, drive first to the Coldwater
Ridge Visitor Center and then drive to the end of Highway 504 at
Johnston Ridge in a total of 43 miles from I-5 at Castle Rock.

Near the Coldwater Ridge Visitor Center, the ¾-mile Winds
of Change Trail, to the right of the entrance of the visitor center,
loops downhill and back up again through an area stripped by

the gravel blast from the Mount St. Helens eruption. The path, overlooking the Toutle River valley, freezes the violence of that instant and, at the same time, illustrates the painfully slow efforts of nature to recover from the blast.

Drive a mile downhill from the visitor center to a boat-launching complex on Coldwater Lake, formed when an avalanche triggered by the mountain's blast blocked the then Coldwater Creek. A trail there leads north above the shore of the lake to a lake access point in 1¼ miles. The trail continues 5½ miles to a junction with trails from the east side of Spirit Lake. Hiking must be confined to trails.

From the end of Highway 504 at the Johnston Ridge Observatory, trails are planned both east and west along the ridge to closer views of the mountain and avalanche damage caused in the eruption.

The ridge is named in memory of David Johnston, a 30-year-old volcanologist with the U.S. Geological Survey, who died on the ridge during the eruption on May 18, 1980, while monitoring disturbances in the mountain from an observation post thought then to be relatively safe.

On his radio, in his last transmission: "Vancouver. Vancouver. This is it!"

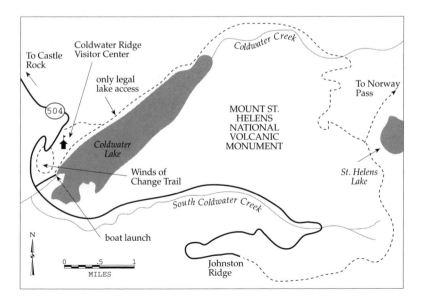

 Horseshoe Creek Falls

Features: forest, river, waterfall
One way: 2 miles and more
Elevation gain: 300 feet
Difficulty: moderate to steep
Open: summer
Map: Green Trails 396

Drop down to one pretty waterfall and then hike on along Siouxon (pronounced "suitson") Creek to views of a much bigger one on Horseshoe Creek. And then....

From I-5 Exit 21 at Woodland, drive east on Highway 503, following it south across the Lewis River at the upper end of Lake Merwin.

At Chelatchie, turn left at a service station/shopping center complex to Road 54. Just beyond the signed entrance into the Gifford Pinchot National Forest, turn left to Road 57 and left again in a short mile to Road 5701 finding the trailhead sign within 100 yards of the end of the road.

Follow the path to Siouxon Creek downhill to the right and across the small noisy waterfall on West Creek in ¼ mile, taking time to rest, tired or not, long enough to soak up the private pleasure of this forest nook.

The path then continues up Siouxon Creek past a junction with the Horseshoe Ridge trail in about a mile and then below dripping cliffs dressed in mosses, ferns, and flowers to the right.

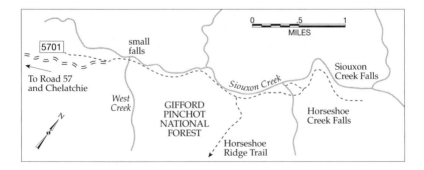

Find Horseshoe Creek Falls at your feet below a bridge over Horseshoe Creek in another long ¼ mile. For a view of the falls from the bottom, take a ¾-mile spur trail beyond the bridge downhill to the left.

Add another mile on the main trail and find yet another waterfall, this one on Siouxon Creek itself, with a large pool surrounded by steplike rocks spread out at its feet.

Falls on Siouxon Creek

 Silver Star Mountain

Features: enormous vistas
One way: 1¼ miles
Elevation gain: 1,000 feet
Difficulty: steep
Open: midsummer
Map: Green Trails 396

Vistas here at 4,390 feet not only of meadows and mountains but of big cities too. After wandering scenic backcountry roads, rough forest roads, and a trail that climbs and climbs.

From I-5 Exit 21 at Woodland, drive east on Highway 503 to Lake Merwin, then follow the highway south to Amboy. At Amboy, turn left onto County Road 12 through the villages of Yacolt and Moulton. (This area is northeast of Battle Ground, north of Vancouver, east of I-5, and south of Mount St. Helens. Use state and Gifford Pinchot forest maps to plot your own way.)

From Moulton, follow County Road 12 along the East Fork of the Lewis River to the Sunset Campground just inside the boundary of the Gifford Pinchot National Forest.

Turn right and cross the river there to Road 41, turning sharply right again in about 3.5 miles onto Road 4109, jolting bump by bump by bump to a parking area at the road's blocked end in about 4 miles. (Roads are so rough here your speedometer is likely to read almost anything.)

The trail follows the road uphill on the side of the mountain across steep flower meadows loaded with bear grass in season. With winds and growing vistas from the west. Near the top, bear

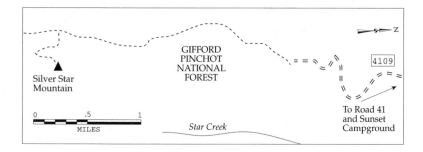

Abandoned road, now a footpath to Silver Star Mountain

left on a spur that climbs sharply to the doorstep (still there) of the long-gone lookout.

From the summit, fantastic views out over Vancouver and Portland. Local hikers make evening treks here on the Fourth of July to watch Portland's fireworks display.

And the mountains? Rainier, Adams, St. Helens, Hood, Jefferson, and even the Olympics.

Beacon Rock trail

 Beacon Rock

Features: river, vista
One way: 1 short mile
Elevation gain: 600 feet
Difficulty: persistent climb
Open: year-round
Maps: Green Trails 428 (Oregon); Forest Trails of the Columbia
    Gorge (Mount Hood National Forest)

Climb fifty-two switchbacks and cross twenty-two bridges to
look out over the Columbia River. With a side trip to waterfalls.
In the Columbia River Gorge National Scenic Area.

From I-5 Exit 7 north of Vancouver, turn onto I-205 and in 10
miles onto Highway 14 along the Washington side of the Columbia River. Beacon Rock State Park in 35 miles.

Find the busy trail up this 800-foot monolith, largest in the United States, off the parking lot on the river side of the highway. The path starts around the rock through trees and then breaks out onto an open rock face and the series of short switchbacks that lead to the top.

The ever-changing scenery and river activity will demand most of your attention as you climb. But take time to note the variety of plants that cling to cracks and crevasses everywhere along the path. From ferns through scotch bells with goats beard, penstemons, and cow parsnips in between.

You'll hear the top before you reach it as the wind whistles through the trees there. From the top: Bonneville Dam to the east, and Crown Point, perched in Oregon high above the Columbia, to the west. And looking down, the most spectacular view of all: a zigzag array of steps and bridges on top of still more steps and bridges. With vultures soaring overhead (mistaking the aroma of struggling hikers for the dead?).

As you'll note, some people run uphill here against time, thankfully their own. Wonder at their choice of this crowded place to test their personal prowess.

Find trails to Rodney and Hardy falls out of the campground and picnic area uphill on the north side of Highway 14. Reach both falls within 1½ miles. Note the Pool of Winds, a large basin scoured in rock below Rodney Falls.

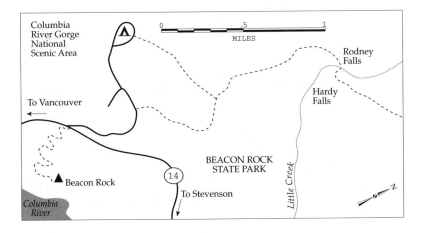

 Wind River Arboretum

Features: story of trees
One way: ½ mile plus
Elevation gain: slight
Difficulty: easy
Open: summer
Map: Green Trails 397

Observe a quiet lesson still being taught after more than eighty years in a "forest" of both the living and dead in an arboretum planted to test the growth of trees from all over the world in a western Washington environment.

From I-5 Exit 7 north of Vancouver, turn onto I-205 and then east in 10 miles to Highway 14 along the Columbia River. Turn north to Carson on the Wind River road, turning left at Stabler crossing, about 6.5 miles north of Carson, to the Wind River Ranger Station.

Or from Randle, on forest roads drive south on Road 25 to Road 90, east on Road 90 to Road 51 (right) up Curly Creek to the Wind River Road 30, turning right (south) to the ranger station.

To find the arboretum, drive to the left across a bridge in front of the ranger station, turning uphill to the right away from the nursery fields between the fourth and fifth houses to a trailhead and parking area.

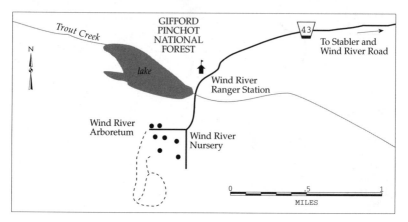

With a brochure from the ranger station, wander trails through the arboretum however you wish, seeking lessons here on the sensitivity of nature and the oft-time futility of man's effort to improve on it.

A collection of 165 conifers from all over the world were planted here beginning in 1912. Many of the transplanted foreign species at first appeared to grow better than trees native to the Northwest, thriving, some of them, for almost forty years before falling victim to seasonal extremes in temperature, rainfalls, etcetera, which varied slightly from those in their native seeding grounds.

Alien broad-leaved and hardwood trees failed entirely. Even trees like Douglas fir, ponderosa pine, lodgepole pine, and western larch transplanted from the Rocky Mountains and eastern Washington fell to diseases that local, native trees survived.

Markers along the trails here show which species died and which trees thrived, demonstrating, if nothing else, that in the long run Nature always knows best.

Wind River Nursery near arboretum

Falls Creek Falls

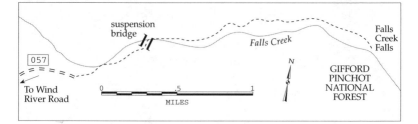

93 Falls Creek Falls

Features: forest, river gorge, waterfall
One way: 2 miles
Elevation gain: 600 feet
Difficulty: easy to moderate
Open: summer
Map: Green Trails 397

Hike across a fern-lined gorge and through rich forest to a three-tiered waterfall on Falls Creek.

From I-5 Exit 7 north of Vancouver, turn onto I-205 and then east in 10 miles to Highway 14 along the Columbia River. Turn north off Highway 14 to Carson on the Wind River Road 30, driving 6.5 miles beyond the ranger station road at Stabler and turning right on Road 3062 (0.5 mile beyond the fork to Government Mineral Springs). In a mile turn right on road 057, driving to the end of the road.

Or from Randle, on forest roads drive south on Road 25 to Road 90, east on Road 90 to Road 51 (right) up Curly Creek to the Wind River Road 30, turning right (south) to Road 3062 (see above).

The trail starts upriver through a clear-cut logged at the turn of the century before entering an old forest. (Note the springboard notches cut in the bigger stumps. Loggers stood on boards jammed into the notches to hand-saw the trees.)

Shortly, the trail crosses a suspension bridge across a narrow, deep, moss- and fern-draped gorge (take time to note the raging river down below) and then makes its way upstream to the base of the waterfall.

(Before crossing the bridge, follow a former trail to picnic and camping spots in lush old forest at a point where the trail once crossed the river.)

Best views of the two tiers of the upper falls about ¼ mile before you reach the pool at the bottom falls. Don't plan to rush away. Such a nice place needs to be enjoyed for awhile.

 Indian Heaven

Features: Indian Heaven lakes, meadows
One way: 2 miles or more
Elevation gain: 800 feet
Difficulty: moderate to steep
Open: summer
Maps: Green Trails 365, 397; Indian Heaven Wilderness

Understand here how this remote plateau earned its name. With far too many lakes to name, too many meadows to note, and too many views of Mount Adams to count, it's heaven and more.

Best in the fall. With huckleberries too. And far fewer bugs.

From I-5 Exit 7 north of Vancouver, turn onto I-205 and then east in 10 miles to Highway 14 along the Columbia River. Drive east to Carson and then north on the Wind River Road (Road 30), turning right in about 5.5 miles (from Highway 14) onto Road 65.

Follow Road 65 to its junction with Road 60 to Trout Lake, continuing on Road 65 another 8.25 miles. Find the trail to the right.

(There are many other ways to reach this country from points within the Gifford Pinchot National Forest. Consult a forest map and pick your own, being careful when you do so to make sure the roads you pick 1) are open and 2) actually go as far as they seem to. Ridges and ranges disrupt roads here in every possible way.)

With a map and compass, plan to spend all the time you've got roaming meadow after meadow to lake after lake—all in the

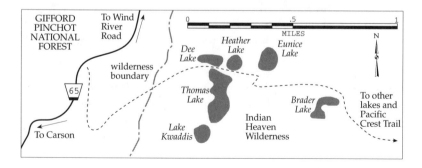

Dee Lake

Indian Heaven Wilderness—while Mount Adams smiles at you in all of the unexpected places.

The trail here climbs from one level of lakes to the next. In ½ mile: Dee Lake on the north side of the trail and Thomas Lake on the south with Heather and Eunice lakes back to the north again.

The path then spurts upward to lush meadows past Brader Lake, just off the trail and over a ridge to the right, and after another sharp climb on to Naha and Rock lakes and Little Rock Lake at the end of 2 miles. With every lake nested in forest, decorated with boulders, and surrounded by meadows filled with berries and color in the fall.

And this is only a sample. In another long mile the trail leads through a plateau of unnamed small lakes and trends downhill past Lake Sahalee Tyee and Blue Lake, biggest of them all, to a junction with the Pacific Crest Trail.

Take care if you leave the trail to seek out any of the dozens of small unnamed lakes all over the place. Unmarked way trails and game trails beckon everywhere. Carry a compass, note the surrounding hills, and keep constant track of where you are and where you've been.

 95 Placid and Chenamus Lakes

Features: forest, lakes, flowers, berries
One way: 2⅕ miles
Elevation gain: 200 feet
Difficulty: moderate
Open: summer
Maps: Green Trails 365; Indian Heaven Wilderness

Sample a succulent corner here of heaven in the Indian Heaven Wilderness with its sparkling lakes, bear grass, huckleberries, and all.

From I-5 Exit 7 north of Vancouver, turn onto I-205 and then east in 10 miles to Highway 14 along the Columbia River. Drive east to Carson and then north on the Wind River Road (Road 30), turning right in about 5.5 miles (from Highway 14) onto Road 65.

Follow Road 65 to its junction with Road 60 to Trout Lake, continuing on Road 65 another 8.25 miles to its end at a junction with Road 30.

Continue ahead on Road 30 about 0.75 mile to turn right on Spur Road 420, finding the trailhead in another mile.

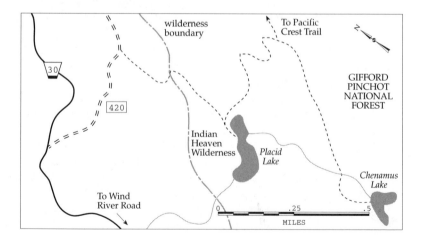

Or, follow Wind River Road 30 north of Carson to its junction with Road 65 in Indian Heaven, bearing left about 0.75 mile to turn right to Spur Road 420. Find the trailhead in another mile.

The path off the right side of the road drops ½ mile gradually through forest to a meadow cove on Placid Lake with picnic and camp spots nearby.

To reach Chenamus Lake, follow a trail to the east along Placid Lake as it turns to the south. The path here climbs 200 feet as it wanders across creeks and through meadows filled with flowers, bear grass, or huckleberries in their season.

Avoid spur trails to the east. Camp spots at Chenamus Lake too.

Placid Lake

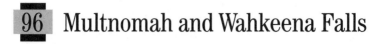 96 Multnomah and Wahkeena Falls

Features: spectacular vistas, spectacular falls
One way: 3½-mile loop
Elevation gain: 800 feet
Difficulty: steep
Open: year-round
Maps: Green Trails 428 (Oregon); Forest Trails of the Columbia
    Gorge (Mount Hood National Forest)

Look up more than 600 feet at one of the most spectacular
waterfalls in the Northwest and then hike away from the crowds
to look down on it and the Columbia River before hiking to a second falls. In the Columbia River Gorge National Scenic Area.

From I-5 Exit 7 north of Vancouver, turn to I-205, cross the
Columbia River, and turn east on I-84 in Oregon. Turn south
from I-84 at Multnomah Falls Exit 31.

Or, for a more interesting drive, turn south off I-84 at Exit 17
to Troutdale and then follow the old Columbia River Scenic
Highway, which climbs past the Crown Point Vista House before
dropping to the clearly marked Multnomah area.

Or, if exploring the north side of the river, cross the Bridge of
the Gods at Cascade Locks, turning west on I-84 and then south
at Exit 35 to the old Columbia River Scenic Highway.

Stand in awe in the presence of the spectacular falls, and
then find the trail to the top beside the Multnomah Falls Lodge
and across the concrete bridge above Lower Multnomah Falls.
Take the trail to the left that switchbacks to the top of the falls.

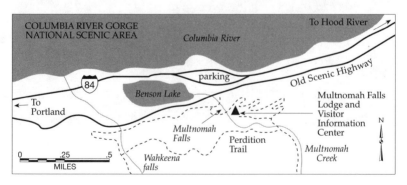

Multnomah Falls

A viewpoint halfway interrupts the tedium of the climb which continues until the trail reaches the top in a mile. Catch your breath and then hike inland, turning sharply downhill to the right in 100 yards or so onto a spur that leads to a viewpoint down on the falls in a few hundred yards.

To continue on to Wahkeena Falls past still more vista points, return to the main trail, cross Multnomah Creek, and turn right to the Perdition Trail.

The way here, living up to its name, clings to the edge of a cliff, high over the gorge, with way trails—if you need them—to even more breathtaking views.

The trail then winds up and down a ridge on a series of log stairways, dropping eventually across the base of Wahkeena Falls and the Wahkeena Falls parking area. To return to Multnomah Falls, take the trail east along the south side of the road.

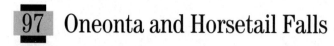 97   Oneonta and Horsetail Falls

Features: forest, waterfalls
One way: 3⅖-mile loop
Elevation gain: 400 feet
Difficulty: moderate to steep
Open: year-round
Maps: Green Trails 428 (Oregon); Forest Trails of the Columbia
  Gorge (Mount Hood National Forest)

Walk into the fern-draped gorge of Oneonta Creek and then hike above it to first one waterfall and then two others, ending at a fourth! In the Columbia River Gorge National Scenic Area.

From I-5 Exit 7 north of Vancouver, turn to I-205, cross the Columbia River, and turn east on I-84 in Oregon. Turn south off I-84 at Exit 17 to Troutdale and the old Columbia River Scenic Highway which climbs past Crown Point Vista House before dropping past the clearly marked Multnomah area and on to the trailhead in 2.2 miles.

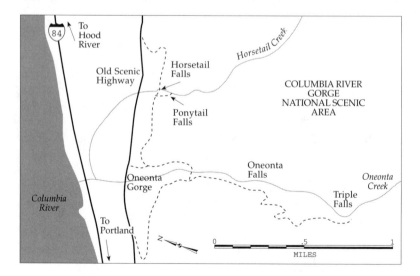

Or, if coming from the north side of the river, cross the Bridge of the Gods at Cascade Locks, turning west on I-84 and then south at Exit 35 to the old Columbia River Scenic Highway.

You'll find no formal trail directly into the Oneonta Creek gorge. In the spring it's often flooded. But in late summer you can pick your way south from the highway up the dry streambed to view the hanging garden of greenery.

Find the formal loop trail to the other waterfalls to the west of the gorge. The loop trail switchbacks first to the west and then back to the east before climbing into a canyon through

Oneonta Creek Gorge

pleasant timber to a junction with the Horsetail Falls Trail in about a mile.

But don't turn left yet. Continue climbing ahead another ¾ mile, switchbacking to the top of Triple Falls. Return then to the Horsetail junction, hiking east over the top of Oneonta Falls to views down on the Columbia River and then back into the canyon behind Ponytail (or Upper Horsetail) Falls. From Ponytail Falls the path drops downhill to Horsetail Falls, ending its loop at the road. Walk west to your car.

Be warned! Leave nothing in your car. Thieves prowl all of these remote parking areas.

98 Punch Bowl Falls

Features: high trail, waterfalls
One way: 2 miles
Elevation gain: about 250 feet
Difficulty: moderate to steep
Open: year-round
Maps: Green Trails 429 (Oregon); Forest Trails of the Columbia
   Gorge (Mount Hood National Forest)

Hike 2 miles above scenic Eagle Creek past one waterfall to
a bowl full of another. In the Columbia River Gorge National
Scenic Area.

From I-5 Exit 7 north of Vancouver, turn to I-205, cross the
Columbia River, and turn east on I-84 in Oregon. Turn south
from I-84 about 1 mile east of Bonneville Exit 40, just beyond the
tunnel, to the Eagle Creek Campground and fish hatchery.

Or, if exploring the north side of the river, cross the Bridge of
the Gods at Cascade Locks, turning west on I-84, looping back to
the east at Bonneville Dam Exit 40, turning to the Eagle Creek
Campground and fish hatchery just beyond the tunnel.

Find the trail at the end of the road beyond the Eagle Creek
picnic area. The path climbs quickly, but never steeply, above the
left side of the creek, eventually making its way along a path
blasted out of a rock cliff, high over the stream.

In about 1½ miles watch for a concrete, ground-level marker
indicating a side trail to a view of Metlako Falls.

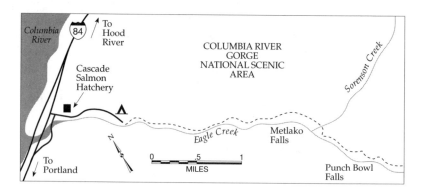

Punch Bowl Falls and Eagle Creek

Beyond Metlako Falls, the trail crosses a stream and then climbs again, reaching a viewpoint above the Punch Bowl at the end of 2 miles. A spur trail leads down to the bowl and the waterfall which seems to leap out of a spout in the cliff.

Be warned! Leave nothing in your car. Thieves prowl all of these remote parking areas.

Sleeping Beauty Trail

99 Sleeping Beauty

Features: forest, vistas
One way: 1⅕ miles
Elevation gain: 1,400 feet
Difficulty: steep
Open: summer
Map: Green Trails 366

Stand on the nose of a basalt lady sleeping beneath a now-tattered coverlet of green. At 4,907 feet, at the end of a not-straight-but-narrow trail that ends in a scenic heaven.

From Trout Lake—about 60 miles south of Randle on Road 23, or 22 miles north of White Salmon and Highway 14—drive west on Highway 141 past the Mount Adams Ranger Station, turning right in less than a mile to Road 88.

In about 4.75 miles, turn right to Road 8810 and right again in another 5-plus miles to Spur Road 040, finding the trailhead on the left in less than 0.5 mile.

(From Randle, drive south on Road 23, beyond the Road 90 junction, turning right on Road 8810 to Spur Road 040.)

(Road 8810 just off Road 88 is signed "NO VEHICLE MAINTE-NANCE BEYOND THIS POINT," but the road to the spur turnoff from the south is practically new.)

The trail starts up through an old clear-cut, becoming a sensible trail shortly as it passes through old hemlock, Douglas fir, and cedars, all giants for the elevation at which they grow amid flowers in season and wild strawberries too on the toe of a rock bluff near the start of the path. The forest becomes more and more open as the trail climbs to the base of the basalt shaft.

At the base of the rock the path proceeds up a carefully built series of switchbacks through scree (avoid wet slabs) to a formal viewpoint just short of the top of the rock. Stop at the signed viewpoint unless you've been instructed and are equipped for the dangers on the slopes beyond.

Views of Mount Adams, Rainier, Hood, and the Trout Lake valley.

The basalt spire is the "nose" of a sleeping beauty that Trout Lake natives say lies across their valley below Mount Adams. Looking northwest from Trout Lake, the beauty lies with her head to the northeast with her body spread out below Adams to the southwest.

Her original coverlet was a lush solid green now sadly patched, ripped, and ragged with clear-cuts and roads.

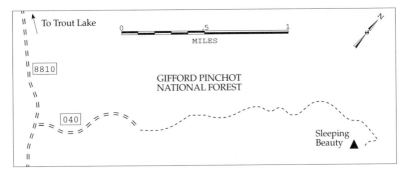

 Langfield Falls

Features: waterfall
One way: ¼ mile
Elevation gain: 100 feet
Difficulty: easy
Open: summer
Map: Green Trails 366

Admittedly, this walk's too short to be a hike, but it leads to a waterfall too grand to be ignored.

From Trout Lake—about 60 miles south of Randle on Road 23, or 22 miles north of White Salmon and Highway 14—drive west on Highway 141 past the Mount Adams Ranger Station, turning right in less than a mile to Road 88.

In about 14 miles, just beyond Tire Junction, marked with a big tractor tire decked with flowers, bear right on Road 88 to a parking area in 0.1 mile on the right.

The path starts out in a cool, pleasant forest, dropping to a formal viewing point and display before continuing to the bottom of the lovely falls with its noisy threads of water here and torrents there. With big rocks to sit on and a pool to admire. A spur path to the right near the beginning of the trail leads to a view down on the falls.

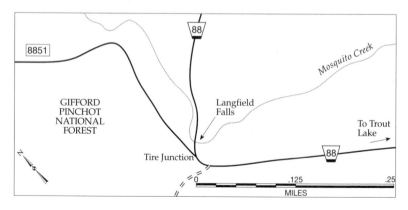

Langfield Falls

The trail was developed in memory of K. C. Langfield, ranger in the Mount Adams district between 1935 and 1956, during a time when the district was still at its pristine best.

101 Steamboat Mountain

Features: forest, berries, vistas
One way: 1 mile
Elevation gain: 800 feet
Difficulty: moderate to steep
Open: summer
Map: Green Trails 366

Flat places, steep places, forest, flowers, a long rocky ridge, ending with a crashing view over the edge of a cliff while all of the great surrounding mountains smile.

From Trout Lake—about 60 miles south of Randle on Road 23, or 22 miles north of White Salmon and Highway 14—drive west on Highway 141 past the Mount Adams Ranger Station, turning right in less than a mile to Road 88.

In about 14 miles, at the Tire Junction marked with a big tire decked with flowers, continue ahead on Road 8851 for 3.3 miles, turning right on Road 8854 and left on Spur Road 021 to a gravel pit. Find the trailhead to the left along the edge of the pit.

The path climbs above the pit and then cuts to the left into forest, turning right shortly to begin a long but pleasant traverse to the ridge along the top of the mountain.

At the ridge the path cuts back to the right, climbing sharply in one final gasp to the former lookout site at the far end of the ridge and almost directly above the place you started.

You won't have been the only visitor here in the summer. Elk seek the windy summit to escape the flies, as all of the elk sign attests.

Flowers in ever-changing displays as you climb this short path, with columbine and huckleberries to start and mariposa lilies (cat's ear lilies) on exposed slopes at the top.

Steamboat Mountain trail

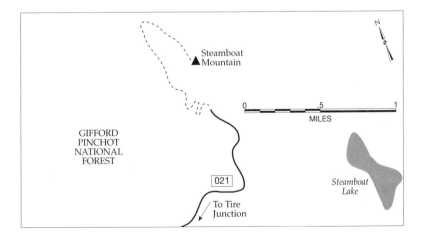

Ice Cave in early summer before vandals break the icicles

102 Ice Cave and Lava Bridges

Features: summer ice and basalt bridges
One way: ¼ mile each
Elevation gain: slight
Difficulty: easy
Open: summer
Map: Green Trails 398

With a flashlight or lantern, climb down to summer ice in a cold lava cave and then hike a sun-drenched loop of lava bridges caused by the same phenomena.

From Trout Lake—about 60 miles south of Randle on Road 23, or 22 miles north of Highway 14 at White Salmon on the Columbia River—drive west on Highway 141 past the Mount

Adams Ranger Station, turning south off Road 24 in about 5.8 miles and following signs to a parking area near the hole-in-the-ground entrance.

A stairway leads into the cave and ice formations to the left of the stairway in a dead-end Crystal Grotto. Although the temperature in the cave is always near freezing, the quality of the ice displays varies from year to year with most of the classic stalactites and stalagmites destroyed by vandals early in the season. A shaft to the right of the entrance stairway leads some 600 feet to an exit. Don't explore it, however, unless you are properly equipped.

To see the lava bridges, return to Road 24, continue west another 0.8 mile, turning left 0.5 mile to a parking area on the right.

A trail to the right leads to two lava bridges that are all that's left of a collapsed lava tube. Cross the first bridge, walk to the right, cross the second, and loop back to where you started. Then cross the first bridge again, turn left to what may be the geological beginning of a still-eroding new bridge-to-be.

The trenches, bridges, and ice cave were formed when molten lava flowed over the area, cooled, and congealed on the outside as the molten lava on the inside continued to flow, leaving a void.

Both the ice caves and the bridges are part of a series of displays marking the exploration of the region by Gen. George McClellan, twice appointed and twice fired by Lincoln as his top general in the Civil War. In 1853, McClellan, with 66 men and 173 horses, passed this way looking for a railroad route over the Cascades.

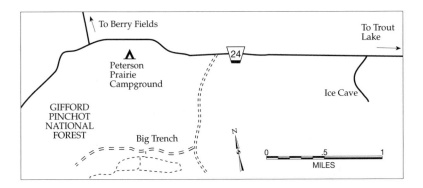

103 Bird and Bluff Lakes Loop

Features: meadows, lakes, waterfalls, flowers
One way: 2½-mile loop
Elevation gain: about 700 feet
Difficulty: moderate
Open: late July
Map: Mount Adams Wilderness

Hike past a waterfall to the edge of Bird Creek Meadows, then through forest and more meadows to Bluff Lake, and then back to Bird Lake. Vistas, vistas, and flowers, flowers everywhere.

A modest day-use fee is sometimes charged.

From Trout Lake—about 60 miles south of Randle on Road 23, or 22 miles north of Highway 14 at White Salmon—drive north from Trout Lake on Road 23, turning right in about a mile to Road 80 and right again in another 0.5 mile onto Road 82.

At the Yakama Indian Reservation boundary, turn left onto reservation Road 184 to Mirror Lake, 15.5 miles from Trout Lake.

At Mirror Lake turn left to Bird Lake and, just beyond a junction with a campground road (to the right), take a short spur to the left, to the trailhead.

(These rough, high roads may be closed some years. Check at the Mount Adams Ranger Station in Trout Lake.)

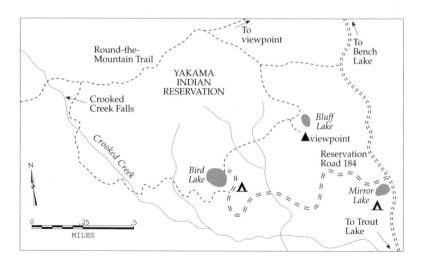

Mount Adams and meadows along Crooked Creek

The path here winds through small meadow after small meadow as it makes its way back and forth up and across Crooked Creek to the base of its waterfall in about a mile. After pictures and time to note the flowers, continue about ¼ mile to a junction with the Round-the-Mountain Trail.

Here, if you have time, turn left toward the Mount Adams Wilderness through glorious meadows and to a point where Crooked Creek earned its name by staggering all over one small meadow.

You'll find some of the best displays of flowers on the windy ridges here where sheep once rested away from flies and deposited seeds of flowers from every part of the Cascades.

To continue your loop trip, return to the trail junction and continue east past a junction with the Trail of Flowers (see hike 104, Bird Creek Meadows).

In ¾ mile, turn right on the downhill path to Bluff Lake, taking time there to follow a shoreline trail to a spectacular cliff-edge view of the Trout Lake valley and Mount Hood to the south.

Find the trail back to Bird Lake Campground off a well-worn area at the end of the small pond that seems tacked onto Bluff Lake. At the campground, follow the road to the left to your car.

One added note: As you walk anywhere here, keep looking back, thus not to miss any surprising view. Mount Adams and Mount Hood lurk everywhere.

Bird Creek Meadows and Mount Adams from Trail of Flowers

104 Bird Creek Meadows

Features: flowers, flowers, vistas, vistas
One way: 1½ miles
Elevation gain: 900 feet
Difficulty: moderate
Open: late summer
Map: Mount Adams Wilderness

U.S. Supreme Court Justice William O. Douglas, who hiked and fished here for years, wrote in *My Wilderness, the Pacific West*: "Bird Creek Meadows seemed like a bit of paradise.... Great blankets of white and pink phlox cover the slopes. Spring beauty and monkey flowers decorate the creek. Indian paintbrush fills every field.... I know of no alpine meadow more rewarding...."

From Trout Lake—about 60 miles south of Randle on Road 23, or 22 miles north of Highway 14 at White Salmon—drive north from Trout Lake on Road 23, turning right in about a mile to Road 80 and right again in another 0.5 mile onto Road 82.

At the boundary of the Yakama Indian Reservation, turn left onto Reservation Road 184, pass Mirror Lake, and in another mile reach a parking area for the Bird Creek Meadows trail, about 16.5

miles from Trout Lake. A modest day-use fee is sometimes charged. (Be warned, these high, rough roads may be closed some years. Check at the Mount Adams Ranger Station in Trout Lake.)

From the parking area, the Round-the-Mountain Trail leads steeply uphill to the west to reach a Trail of Flowers. Take this loop to the right, through what may be the largest assortment of alpine wild flowers in the world. More than 400 varieties pour out over these meadows in streams of color from mid-July until mid-September, blooming at their peak in mid-August.

The flower trail climbs sharply to a higher ridge and then circles to the left before dropping back to where you started. With two side trips en route.

At the height of the loop, follow a faint path to the right toward Mount Adams across dry and drier slopes and past wind-shaped alpine trees and small clinging clumps of flowers to a cliff-edge overlooking Hellroaring Meadows (hike 105), the Mazama Glacier, and a noisy mountainside of waterfalls.

(From the overlook you can return to the loop or hike downhill following rocks and cairns along the rim of the gorge to the Round-the-Mountain Trail about 100 yards from the parking lot.)

If you return from the overlook to the flower trail, consider taking time to turn right on the Round-the-Mountain Trail and walk toward the Mount Adams Wilderness and the appropriately named Crooked Creek (see hike 103, Bird and Bluff Lakes Loop.)

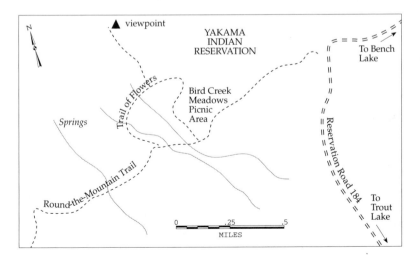

 Hellroaring Meadows

Features: meadows, forest, a spring, a lake
One way: 1 mile
Elevation gain: slight
Difficulty: easy to moderate
Open: late summer
Map: Mount Adams Wilderness

Acres of verdant, soggy mountain meadows with their own small private lake—all under the watchful eye of towering Mount Adams.

From Trout Lake (about 60 miles south of Randle on Road 23, or 22 miles north of Highway 14 at White Salmon on the Columbia River), drive north from Trout Lake on Road 23, turning right in about a mile to Road 80 and right again in another 0.5 mile onto Road 82.

At the boundary of the Yakama Indian Reservation, turn left onto Reservation Road 184, pass Mirror Lake and the trailhead to Bird Creek Meadows, driving another 0.6 mile to a helicopter landing area, viewpoint, and trailhead on the left, about 17 miles from Trout Lake. A modest day-use fee is sometimes charged here.

(Be warned, these high, rough roads may be closed some years. Check at the Mount Adams Ranger Station in Trout Lake.)

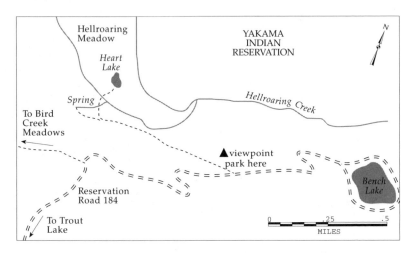

A gentle 1½-mile trail from the viewpoint leads toward Mount Adams through pretty forest ending on the edge of the big meadow at a spring where a small creek bubbles full blown from the rocks at your feet. Flowers everywhere with every species blossoming wildly in its season.

Wander where you will but wander for sure to Heart Lake, hiding on a low bench to the north, ¼ mile from the trail.

To find the lake, walk toward and beyond a Heart Lake sign in the meadow to the north at the end of the trail. Follow way-paths cross-country, hopping or wading a stream if you can't find a log, to a path leading to the top of the bench and the lake, to the north, in the trees.

At the lake: rock slabs for picnics and naps, glimpses of Adams, and lots and lots of privacy. Swimming if you're brave. And expect to spend at least an hour more than you planned. You'll find it hard to say goodbye.

Mount Adams from Hellroaring Meadows

Appendix: Campgrounds
Highway 101

Hikes 1–2

Potlatch State Park. 35 sites including 18 trailer units in open area on Hood Canal. Oysters and clams at low tide. Rest rooms. Piped water. Fee. 3 miles south of Hoodsport.

Lake Cushman State Park. 81 sites with 30 hookups in a wooded area away from the lake. Rest rooms. Piped water. Fee. 7 miles west of Hoodsport.

Big Creek. 23 sites on forested loops in national forest. Toilets. Water. Fee. West of Hoodsport at the junction with Road 24.

Staircase. 59 sites on pleasant forest loops. Some along the river. In Olympic National Park. Rest rooms. Piped water. Fee. 19 miles west of Hoodsport.

Hikes 3–4

Elkhorn. 18 sites in a very pleasant forest on the Dosewallips River. Many sites on river. Toilets. Water. Fee. 11 miles west of Brinnon on Road 2610.

Dosewallips. 30 sites in open big timber. Sites along the river. Not recommended for trailers, entry road is too steep. Rest rooms. Piped water. 15 miles from Brinnon at the end of Road 2610.

Seal Rock. 35 sites on wooded loops on Hood Canal. All away from the water. Only Forest Service campground in the nation with oyster-picking opportunities. Rest rooms. Piped water. Fee. 2 miles north of Brinnon on Highway 101.

Hikes 5–6

Falls View. 35 sites in rhododendron forest. Rest rooms. Piped water. 4 miles south of Quilcene on Highway 101.

Sequim Bay State Park. 86 sites in heavily used area on bluff above Sequim Bay. Rest rooms. Piped water. Fee. 4 miles southeast of Sequim.

Hike 7

Fort Worden State Park. 80 sites, some on open loops near Strait of Juan de Fuca and Admiralty Inlet. Reservations available. Rest rooms. Piped water. Fee. In the northeastern corner of Port Townsend. A former military reservation.

Hike 8

See Sequim Bay State Park, hikes 5–6.

Hike 9

Dungeness Recreation Area. 65 sites on high bluff loops near Dungeness Spit. Some in trees. Some in open. A Clallam County Park. Rest rooms. Water. Fee.

Hike 10

Deer Park. 18 sites in beautiful alpine setting surrounded by meadows at 5,400 feet. Toilets. Piped water from spring. Fee. 17 miles from Highway 101 over narrow, steep mountain road. Not suitable for trailers.

Hikes 11–13

Heart of the Hills. 105 sites on a series of forest loops. A pleasant area. Sites well separated. Rest rooms. Piped water. Campfire programs. Fee. 5.4 miles from Port Angeles.

Hikes 14–15

Fairholm. 87 sites. Some walk-in tent sites near the lake. Most on wooded loops. Rest rooms. Piped water. Campfire programs. Fee. At the west end of Lake Crescent.

Hike 16

Sol Duc. 80 sites in two campgrounds. Sites in thinned timber in the first campground off the Sol Duc Road. Sites in natural timber setting in the second campground. Rest rooms. Piped water. Campfire programs. Fee. Hot-spring resort nearby.

Klahowya. 55 sites in rich forest setting along the Sol Duc River. Many near the river. Toilets. Piped water. Fee. Nature trail. About 9 miles west of Lake Crescent on Highway 101.

Hikes 17–19

Ozette Lake. 14 primitive sites on open loop on Ozette Lake. Rest rooms and water nearby. Open year-round.

Hikes 20–23

Mora. 94 sites on deeply shaded forest loops. Rest rooms. Piped water. Campfire programs. Fee. Nature trails. Beachcombing nearby. Some facilities open in winter. Turn west 2 miles north of Forks. 11.9 miles from Highway 101.

Hikes 24–25

Hoh. 89 sites on beautiful rain-forest loops near the Hoh River. Rest rooms. Piped water. Campfire programs. Nature trails. Fee. Turn east 14 miles south of Forks. 19 miles from Highway 101.

Hikes 26–27

Kalaloch. 177 sites on wooded loops on bluff above ocean beach. Some sites overlooking beach. A crowded campground in summer and on some winter weekends. Forest walks. Beachcombing. Rest rooms. Piped water. Campfire programs. Fee.

Hike 28

Queets River. 20 tent-only sites in rain-forest setting on Queets River. Toilets. No drinking water. Turn left to Queets River road about 6 miles south of Queets or about 8 miles south of Olympic National Park beach strip boundary. 14 miles on dirt road from Highway 101. A primitive area.

Hike 29

July Creek. 29 tent sites on the north side of Quinault Lake. Walk-in sites above the lake. No trailers. No recreation use of the lake from the camp. Lake is part of the Quinault Indian Reservation. Piped water. Rest rooms. Fee. 3.9 miles from Highway 101.

Willaby. 21 sites on Quinault Lake. Some sites on lake, others in timber. Rest rooms. Piped water. Fee.

Falls Creek. 31 sites on Quinault Lake, most on timbered loops. Rest rooms. Piped water. Fee.

Graves Creek. 30 sites on a single loop in quiet forest. Rest rooms. Water. Fee. 20 miles from Highway 101.

Chinook Pass Highway 410

Hikes 30–32

Ipsut Creek. 29 sites on loop in pleasant forest. Busy on weekends. Evening programs on weekends. Rest rooms. Pit toilets. Piped water. Fee. 18 miles from Wilkeson.

Hikes 33–34

Mowich Lake. Hikers' camp on open loop. No formal sites. Water. Toilets.

Hikes 35–38

The Dalles. 44 sites on forested loops, some near the White River. Toilets. Water. Fee. 25 miles from Enumclaw.

Silver Springs. 20 units in open timber. Spring in middle of camp. Piped water. Toilets. Fee. 31 miles from Enumclaw.

Corral Pass. 20 sites in subalpine setting at 5,700 feet. Toilets. No fee. 6 miles from Highway 410 on Corral Pass Road 7140. Too steep for trailers.

Hikes 39—45

White River. 117 sites on wooded loops. A few with views of Mount Rainier from sites above the White River. Piped water. Rest rooms. Evening programs. Fee. Off Highway 410, 5 miles beyond the White River entrance station to Mount Rainier National Park.

Sunrise. 10-unit hikers' camp about 1.2 miles from the Sunrise parking lot. One of the few camps in the state at this elevation. Usually closed by snow until mid-July. Always chilly at night. Water. Rest rooms. Trail from Sunrise parking lot 14.5 miles from the White River entrance station.

Hike 46

See White River, hikes 39–45; and Ohanepecosh, hikes 62–64.

Hikes 47—48

Lodgepole. 32 sites in open lodgepole pine. Some sites oriented to the river. Toilets. Well water. Fee. 8.3 miles from Chinook Pass.

Pleasant Valley. 14 sites in flat open area south of Highway 410. Heavy trailer use. Toilets. No water. 11.8 miles from Chinook Pass.

Hells Crossing. 17 sites well-separated in open timber. Carry gear to table and tent sites. Toilets. Water. Fee. 15 miles from Chinook Pass.

Also see White River, hikes 39–45.

Hike 49

Deep Creek. 6 sites on deep forest loop at the end of Road 1808. Toilets. No fee. About 20 miles from Highway 410.

Cedar Springs. 15 sites in open forest. Some along the Bumping River. Toilets. Water. Fee. 0.75 mile south of Highway 410 on Bumping River Road.

Soda Springs. 19 sites in pleasant timber along the Bumping River. Most near the river. Toilets. Well water. Fee. 4.8 miles from Highway 410.

Bumping Dam. 31 units on flat wooded area below Bumping Dam. Drive over the top of the dam to reach the campground. Toilets. Water. Fee. 11.4 miles from Highway 410.

Hike 50

Little Naches. 17 sites near Highway 410 at the Little Naches Road junction. Heavy trailer use. Toilets. Fee.

Kaner Flats. 42 units. Picnic area on river. Toilets. Well water. Fee. 2.3 miles north of Highway 410 on Road 197.

Sawmill Flat. 27 sites, most for trailers. Toilets. Well water. Fee. 6.7 miles north of Naches Ranger Station.

Cottonwood. 16 sites in cottonwood brake. Toilets. Well water. Fee. 7 miles north of Naches Ranger Station.

Highways 7 and 706

Hikes 51—52

Big Creek. 30 sites in national forest just outside Mount Rainier National Park. Toilets. Water. Fee. Turn south off Highway 706, the road to the Nisqually entrance of the park, onto Road 52 about 3 miles west of the park entrance. In about 1.5 miles turn east to the campground in 0.5 mile.

Sunshine Point. 18 sites on a lightly timbered bar on the Nisqually River. Toilets. Water. Fee. About 0.2 mile from the Nisqually entrance station.

Hikes 53—57

Cougar Rock. 200 sites on forest loops. Rest rooms. Piped water. Evening programs. Fee. 8 miles from Nisqually entrance.

Stevens Canyon Road

Hikes 58–64

Ohanapecosh. 205 units on pleasant wooded loops. Some walk-in sites near the Ohanapecosh River. Rest rooms. Piped water. Evening programs. Often full on weekends. Fee. 1.5 miles south of the Stevens Canyon entrance to Mount Rainier National Park on Highway 123.

White Pass Highway 12

Hike 65

Clear Lake. 61 sites in camps on both sides of the outlet of Clear Lake. Some near the river below the Clear Lake dam. Toilets. Water. 1.25 miles off Highway 12 and Road 1200 on Spur Road 740.

Hike 66

La Wis Wis. 100 sites on forest loops near the Ohanapecosh River. Rest rooms. Water. Fee. Busy on weekends. About 0.25 mile south of intersection of Highways 12 and 123 southeast of Mount Rainier National Park.

Randle–Trout Lake Road 23

Hikes 67–70

Tower Rock. 22 sites on Cispus River. Most oriented to the water. A damp cottonwood/cedar area. Toilets. Water. Fee. Below Tower Rock. Off Road 76 on Road 2306.

North Fork. 33 sites on forest loops. Toilets. Water. Fee. Guard station. Off Road 23 about 0.5 mile east of junction with Road 22.

Hike 71

Blue Lake Creek. 11 sites in hardwood glade surrounded by meadow. Trail to Cispus River. Toilet. Water. Fee. North of Road 23 beyond North Fork Campground.

Adams Fork. 24 sites in parklike stand of fir. Sites back from the Cispus River. Swimming. Toilets. Water. Fee. On Road 21 beyond turnoff of Road 23.

Hikes 72–73

Takhlakh. 54 sites on a pleasant wooded loop on Takhlakh Lake. No sites directly on the lake. Toilets. Water. Fee. From Road 23 (from Randle) turn left on Road 1095 (near Baby Shoe Pass) and right in a mile to Road 2329.

Council Lake. 10 sites on a loop above Council Lake. A rough, steep campground road. Primarily a fishing camp. Toilet. No water. No fee. Off Road 23, about a mile south of Baby Shoe Pass, to Road 2334. Campground within a mile.

Randle–Mount St. Helens Road 25

Hikes 74–79

Iron Creek. 98 sites on loops in beautiful ancient forest. Some sites near Iron Creek and Cispus River. Water. Toilets. Fee. Near junction of Roads 25 and 76 south of Randle.

Also see Tower Rock, hikes 67–70.

Pole Patch. 12 sites at 4,400 feet in light subalpine trees. Views of nearby peaks from ridge above the camp. No water. Toilets. Busy during huckleberry season. On Road 77. A steep climb from the valley.

Highway 503 and Road 90

Hikes 80–83

Cougar. 38 tent-only sites in a camp maintained by Pacific Power and Light Co. Rest rooms. Water. On Yale reservoir about 14 miles east of Yale on Road 90.

Swift. 90 sites on wooded loops near Swift Creek reservoir. Operated by Pacific Power and Light Co. Rest rooms. Water. Turn off Road 90 about 0.1 mile below the ranger station.

Hikes 84–87

Lower Falls Recreation Area. 42 sites in forested area near waterfalls on the Cispus River. Toilets. Water. Pleasant but busy. On Road 90, 14.2 miles east of junction with Road 25, or 16 miles on Road 90 from Road 23 at Baby Shoe Pass.

Spirit Lake Memorial Highway 504

Hike 88

Lewis and Clark State Park. 25 tent sites 12 miles southeast of Chehalis. Rest rooms. Water. Closed October through March. Turn east from I-5 onto Highway 12 at Exit 68 about 10 miles south of Chehalis and then right in 1 mile to Jackson Highway. Campground in about another mile.

Seaquest State Park. 90 sites in wooded area near Mount St. Helens National Volcanic Monument Visitor Center. Water. Rest rooms. 16 sites with utilities. 5 miles east of Castle Rock on Highway 504. Exit I-5 at Exit 49.

Highway 503

Hikes 89–90

See Cougar, hikes 80–83.

Sunset. 16 sites in forest along the East Fork of the Lewis River. Toilets. Water. Fee. South of Highway 503 at Amboy through Yacolt to Road 12. At boundary of Gifford Pinchot National Forest.

Battleground Lake State Park. 35 sites on Battleground Lake. Rest rooms. Water. Fee. Northeast of Highway 503 at Battleground.

Highway 14

Hike 91

Beacon Rock State Park. 33 sites on forest loops away and above the highway. Rest rooms. Water. Fee. Across Highway 14 from Beacon Rock.

Hikes 92–93

Panther Creek. 33 sites in young forest near Panther Creek. Toilets. Water. Fee. 10 miles from Carson on Road 65.

Beaver. 24 sites near Government Mineral Springs. Some sites on the Wind River. Toilets. Water. Fee. 12 miles from Carson on Road 30.

Paradise Creek. 42 sites on parklike loops near Wind River. Toilets. Water. Fee. 20 miles from Carson on Road 30.

Hikes 94–95

See Paradise Creek, hikes 92–93.

Goose Lake. 25 sites on loop above Goose Lake. Most on a steep hillside. Toilets. Water. Fee. South of Indian Heaven Wilderness. On Road 60 about 12.7 miles from Trout Lake. About 16.7 miles from Carson via Road 65.

Little Goose. 28 sites in timber. Toilets. Water. Fee. East of Indian Heaven Wilderness. Popular with berry pickers. On Road 24, 0.3 mile from Trout Lake.

Cultus Creek. 51 sites on loops in open canopy of trees. Toilets. Water. Fee. East of Indian Heaven Wilderness. 17.5 miles from Trout Lake.

Tillicum. 49 sites on timber loops. Toilets. Water. Fee. North of Indian Heaven Wilderness. On Road 24 about 2 miles north of junction with Road 30 from Carson. 24 miles from Trout Lake.

Note: Indian campgrounds east of Indian Heaven Wilderness are closed to the general public.

Interstate 84

Hikes 96–98

Eagle Creek. 20 sites on forested bluff above the Columbia River. Rest rooms. Water. Fee. (See Hike 98 for directions.)

Ainsworth. 45 sites on open grassy loop. Rest rooms. Water. Fee. About 3.5 miles east of Multnomah Falls on the old Columbia River Scenic Highway.

Forest Road 88

Hikes 99–102

Peterson Prairie. 30 sites near stream in pleasant timbered area. Toilets. Water. Fee. 7.4 miles west of Trout Lake on Road 24.

Trout Lake Creek. 21 sites in rich forest near Trout Lake Creek. Toilets. No water. No fee. Off Roads 88 and 8810 on Spur Road 011.

See Tillicum, hikes 94–95.

Forest Roads 23 and 80

Hikes 103–105

Mirror Lake. 7 sites on small lake at 5,300 feet. Toilets. Water. Fee. Busy and often dusty.

Bird Lake. 20 sites at 5,500 feet in open timber. Toilets. Water. Fee. Some with views of Mount Adams. West of Mirror Lake.

Bench Lake. 34 sites on loop around Bench Lake. Toilets. Water. Fee. At the end of the road beyond Bird Creek Meadows.

Reading Suggestions

Wilderness Travel

Graydon, Don, ed. *Mountaineering, The Freedom of the Hills* (5th ed.). Seattle: The Mountaineers, 1992.

Manning, Harvey. *Backpacking: One Step at a Time.* New York: Vintage Books, 1985.

Sterling, E. M. *Best Short Hikes in Washington's Cascades & San Juan Islands.* Seattle: The Mountaineers, 1994.

Trees and Flowers

Arno, Stephen F., and Hammerly, Ramona P. *Northwest Trees.* Seattle: The Mountaineers, 1977.

Lyons, C. P. *Trees, Shrubs and Flowers to Know in Washington.* Vancouver, B.C.: J. M. Dent & Sons, Ltd.

Manning, Harvey. *Mountain Flowers.* Seattle: The Mountaineers, 1979.

Nature Guides

Kozloff, Eugene N. *Plants and Animals of the Pacific Northwest.* Seattle: University of Washington Press.

Peterson, Roger Tory. *A Field Guide to Western Birds.* Boston: Houghton Mifflin Co.

Whitney, Stephen R. *A Field Guide to the Cascades and Olympics.* Seattle: The Mountaineers, 1983.

Index

About the Author

E. M. Sterling has written four other books published by The Mountaineers: *The South Cascades,* a critique of the management of Northwest forests, which went out of print when Mount St. Helens covered up the evidence; two forest trail guides—*Trips and Trails 1* and *2*; and the companion volume to this book: *Best Short Hikes in Washington's North Cascades and San Juan Islands.*

About the Photographers

Twin brothers Bob and Ira Spring's crisp, breathtaking images of the Northwest wilderness have been inspiring outdoor enthusiasts for several decades. Their creative stamp can be found in more than forty books on the outdoors, including The Mountaineers' *100 Hikes in* series. One of the Northwest's most active trail lobbyists, Ira Spring was given the 1992 Theodore Roosevelt Conservation Award by Congressman John Miller for his volunteer efforts toward trail preservation and funding.